LIFE CHANGES
JAMES C. HEFLEY

Tyndale House Publishers, Inc.
Wheaton, Illinois

Front cover photo by Lamar Smith

First printing, January 1984
Library of Congress Catalog Card Number 83-50676
ISBN 0-8423-2155-1, paper
Copyright © 1984 by James C. Hefley
All rights reserved
Printed in the United States of America

For Marti

With Whom

I intend

lovingly to spend

the

rest of my life

Contents

O N E
The Accident That Changed My Life 9

T W O
Bogged Down at Forty or Fifty 21

T H R E E
Out of a Job... or About to Be 45

F O U R
When Adversity Strikes 71

F I V E
When You Lose a Spouse 93

S I X
Early Retirement 123

S E V E N
Hanging It Up at Sixty-five 145

E I G H T
Getting "Way Up There" 171

1

The Accident That Changed My Life

It was a cold and foggy February day on our Tennessee mountain—all the more dreary because I had just returned from a week of research in sunny southern California. The weather had been delightful, the news of three old friends less so. One, whom I had expected to interview, was in the hospital dying from acute leukemia. The other two, a couple, had said they were getting a divorce. I was astounded. On a previous trip I was in their home and they were telling about the new book they had written together on how to have a happy marriage. This and the weather waiting at home did not exactly make me want to dance in the street.

I plumped down into my favorite chair, a big, black, wraparound recliner that sat before the fireplace in the family room. My daughters and several other young people were in the room. I paid no attention to their chattering. Neither did they appear to notice me. Maybe they thought I was hibernating. After being on the plane all night from Los Angeles to Atlanta and catching the daylight flight to Chattanooga, I felt like taking a deep sleep for the rest of the winter.

The room was cold. The fire was down to a few smoldering coals. Wearily, I got up and brought a few sticks of wood from the garage, then slumped back into the chair. When the wood didn't catch, I got up again and began raking coals from the back of the fireplace. I had my head halfway in, when—boom! a firecracker exploded just under my right ear. Bells started ringing in my head.

"Ooops, sorry about that," said the young man behind me. "It was left over from Christmas. I tossed it in there while you were in the garage. I thought it would go off before you got back."

"No harm done," I muttered and fell back into the chair. But the sound, now a steady monotonous ring, was still there. I got up and took a drive down the mountain. I could hear the ringing above the car motor.

I didn't say anything to Marti until we were in bed that night and she asked, "Why do you have your head so close to the radio?"

"I'm trying to drown out the ringing in my ears." Then I told her about the firecracker.

"Relax and put your mind on something else. Me, for instance. Everybody hears some noise."

"But not like this," I grumped.

She turned over and went to sleep.

When the ringing didn't go away, I made an appointment to see an ear, nose, and throat physician—a man who was a lay leader at a church we had once attended.

"Good," Marti said when I told her. "He'll probably find you've just got wax in your ears."

The doctor's office was across the street from Erlanger Hospital. "First the exam," the nurse-receptionist said as she whisked me into a little soundproof room.

A white-coated attendant peered at me from the other side of a glass. "Tell me 'yes' or 'no' when you hear something," he said and began testing me on beeping tones that steadily sounded farther and farther away. Then he checked me on the pitch scale and concluded with a list of words—first in one ear, then in the other.

The doctor frowned over the squiggly lines on

my charts. "Hmmm. Hmmm. Well, you do have a problem. You have a pronounced hearing loss in your right ear, and a slight loss in the other: both in your ability to hear sounds and to catch the high frequencies. I'd say it's nerve deafness and will get worse. In fifteen years you may be in real difficulty."

"Oh, have you been shooting a gun lately?" he added as a seeming afterthought.

I told him about the firecracker.

"Well, that might have contributed," he said.

"I also have a very annoying ringing in my ears."

"You do? Well, nothing we can do about that either. You'd just better pray it will go away. Anything else?"

When I shook my head, he picked up his dictaphone and read the whole gloomy litany back, throwing in a few technical words which I didn't understand. I walked back to the reception room, paid the forty-dollar bill, and went out feeling worse than when I had come in.

Back home, I was intent on proving that I really wasn't going deaf. Every time someone spoke, I strained to catch every syllable. But the ringing wouldn't go away. I couldn't concentrate. All I could hear was the discordant sound and the doctor saying, "You do have a problem . . . in fifteen years. . . ."

There was a stream a couple of miles away. I packed research notes and writing materials into my attaché case and went to sit by a small waterfall. The roar of the water muffled the ringing. It was great until I left.

The encyclopedia told me more than the doctor. Nerve deafness, the article said, could be inherited. "I got it from Grandpa Foster," I moaned to Marti. "His hearing started to go bad at about my age" (I was then forty-seven). "By sixty-five, he was so deaf we had to shout in his ears."

"You don't know that you have nerve deafness," Marti declared. "You don't know that you'll be like your grandfather."

Nothing she could say alleviated my worry. I remembered that in later life Grandpa had become almost a hermit. Once he had told me, "I don't want to go anywhere because I don't understand anything people say. I'm just a bother." I remembered having to shout in his ear. "What's that again?" he would answer back, and I would have to shout louder.

In fifteen years, maybe sooner, would I be like Grandpa?

How could I continue to work? Travel? Interview people for articles and books? What editor would give an assignment to a deaf writer? How would the mortgage be paid? Could we send our two daughters still at home to college?

Moan, groan, gripe, complain. *What am I going to do for the rest of my life? How can I live with growing deafness? How can I put up with this infernal ringing?*

During college I had followed the Navigator system for Scripture memorizing. Comforting verses began coming back, such as:

"Trust in the Lord with all thine heart; and lean not unto thine own understanding. In all thy ways acknowledge him, and he shall direct thy paths" (Proverbs 3:5, 6).

"My God shall supply all your need according to his riches in glory by Christ Jesus" (Philippians 4:19).

"The Lord has provided for us before," Marti said, "and he will continue to in the future. Don't you think he will?"

"Yes, yes," I replied, but with no feeling of confidence.

I went into my study and tried to work. The creative juices refused to flow. I stared through the window at the bleak, leafless trees. I returned to the big, black chair and sat staring into the now cold fireplace. I had found something else to stew about: *I'll be forty-eight years old my next birthday. In nineteen years I'll be as old as Dad is now. My life is almost over and what have I accomplished?*

I had been a full-time writer for fourteen years, an editor and a pastor before that. Actually, I had a lot to thank God for.

Many people had told me, "I envy you. You're free to live where you wish. Write whatever you like." But at that time I didn't *feel* that my life had counted for very much. My books hadn't sold in the millions. I wasn't a household name. I had spent too much time closeted away from my family, churning out mediocrity. I had robbed my family of companionship. My children were almost grown and I couldn't make up the past. We were just treading water financially. Just managing to pay the bills and not getting ahead.

The future looked dull and gray. What else was there to do but more of the same? *Ten years from now I'll be where I am now, except more deaf. Is this what I want to do for the rest of my life?*

Now I realize that I was suffering from exhaustion and mild depression, combined with symptoms of a midlife crisis. Dr. James Mallory later told me when I was helping him with a book:

> A depressed person thinks differently and much more negatively. It's as if a black filter is drawn over perceptions of the past and future. He has a tendency to go back through the past and excessively ruminate about all real or imagined wrongs: "My whole life has been a failure. I've never been anything else." He keeps building a case against himself, adjudicating himself guilty and worthless (*Untwisted Living*, Victor Books, 1982, p. 79).

My situation certainly wasn't as dark as I thought. My mind had exaggerated the minuses to such an extent that I couldn't see the pluses. It was a good case of selective perception.

I later learned that I couldn't have inherited my Grandpa Foster's deafness. "Don't you know?" my sister Louise said when I asked her. "Grandpa said his deafness was caused from working on the railroad. I've never heard of inherited deafness in our family."

An otologist in Nashville examined me thoroughly and found no evidence of nerve deafness. The firecracker, he said, had probably caused my hearing impairment. It was something I could live with and which need not get worse. "Millions of people hear a ringing in their ears," he added. "You can get used to that." And I have. Most of the time now I don't even think of it.

The episode turned out to be one of the best experiences of my life as I went on to answer the question, "What am I going to do with the rest of my life?"

One result of my midlife trauma was that I saw —really saw—*others* caught in wrenching difficulties, struggling with this same question. Men and women in midlife caught in a morass of negativism. People who felt themselves trapped in a dead-end job. Some out of work with little hope of ever obtaining a fulfilling job. Divorced and widowed individuals, struggling to build new identities. Others experiencing adversity and wondering if anything was left worth living for. Still others facing retirement or old age without any challenging purpose for the rest of their lives. Awareness of these fellow strugglers fueled my desire to write this book.

My friend Bert was only a couple of years short of fifty-five, but he sounded seventy-five when he answered the phone. I called him during a stopover on a business trip along the East Coast. "I lost my job three months ago," he said immediately. "Harriet has been sick in the hospital. The kids are giving me trouble...."

I had known Bert for thirty years and could never remember a time when he was not employed. He had a master's degree and outstanding skills as an analyst in the steel industry. I didn't quite know what to say.

"My company was bought out by a syndicate," he explained. "They decided to close the office where I was working. Gave their salaried employees only a month's severance pay."

Bert was still jobless the next time I called him. His finances were in bad shape. "We're close to losing both cars," he admitted. "The utility company is threatening to turn off our heat.

"Here I am, fifty-five years old, at a time when I should be in the prime of a good career and putting away a nest egg for retirement. Now I don't know if I have any future. I even tried to get a job pumping gas. The guy said I was overqualified."

While Bert's predicament was still fresh in my mind, Marti got a call from a neighbor woman whose children had left the nest. Now she had a big house and executive husband to pamper. "I'm at my wit's end," she said. "I don't know what I'm going to do."

"What's the problem?" Marti asked.

The words came gushing out. "Bill came home one night last week and out of the clear blue said he didn't love me anymore. Just like that. After thirty-two years and five kids he doesn't love me. I was so shocked I couldn't speak. Finally, I said, 'Didn't you love me when we got married?' 'Yes,' he admitted. 'What have I done to make you quit loving me?' 'Nothing,' he said. 'Nothing that I know of. I'm just tired of you, that's all. I want a little excitement.' Just like that," she told Marti. "I had no idea he felt this way. No warning.

"He's willing to give me the house and a good

financial settlement. Plus alimony. I can't make him stay. I can't prove it, but I think he's got his secretary in an apartment. What am I going to do?"

A few weeks later she told us that the divorce was going through. The children had sided with her. "They can't stand their father. They telephone me every day. But they have their own lives to live, while I have nothing left. I'm fifty-five years old, too young to give up and die. All I've ever done is keep house, care for a husband, and raise kids. What am I going to do in the future?"

We had moved to Signal Mountain just ten years before—a lovely mountain suburb of Chattanooga, just 6,000 in population. It is a community of churches with a country club and neighborliness, where crime is little known. And of hard-working, success-chasing husbands who seem to be dying too rapidly.

We arrived about the time a neighbor, active in our church, collapsed and died on the golf course. Still in his forties, he had a bright path before him. We saw his wife struggling to break through the gloom, keep her family together, and get on with the rest of her life.

A couple of years later another fine, church-going husband who lived just down the street had a fatal coronary. Same sad song for his widow.

Our next-door neighbor, a just-retired FBI agent, was next. Then the garage owner who lived straight across the street from us. One morning I saw him backing out of the driveway to go to work. The next day he died from a heart attack while on a fishing trip.

Both left grieving widows who have had to answer the same difficult question: "What am I going to do with the rest of my life?"

Not long ago I was talking to a young father. A former all-star college athlete, Larry had had everything going for him: Engaged to marry a beautiful girl. A comfortable five-figure corporate salary. Driving home from Nashville, he fell asleep and his car ran off the road. The doctors at the hospital said he was only dazed from a mild concussion and would be going home in a couple of days. How it happened, Larry still doesn't know, but somehow he fell through the window of his second-floor hospital room. The fall shattered a vertebra in his spine, paralyzing him from the waist down.

Larry went home in a wheelchair, knowing he would probably be unable to walk for the rest of his life.

To make matters worse, Larry's fiancée broke their engagement and he also lost his job. Larry, however, had one big plus going for him. He was a Christian. Through faith and sheer grit he made it. He is still paralyzed, but he now has a good job and a loving, devoted wife—a girl he met after his accident. "It was tough for awhile," Larry admitted. "I just didn't know what was to become of me."

During the last few years I've met others, like Larry, who have been hit by adversity. One friend had a stroke. One day, the picture of health; the next, battling for his life in intensive care. Another was felled in midlife by a heart attack. After unsuccessful surgery, his doctor informed him, "You have at best a year to live." What was he to do for the rest of his life?

After turning fifty I began paying closer attention to friends making the transition in retirement. I asked a doctor friend who was preparing to put away his stethoscope, "What are your plans?"

"That's a good question," he replied. "Geri and I have a lot of ideas, but we haven't settled on anything definite yet."

I spent the night with an accountant and his wife in New Jersey—old friends from many years back. "My number is coming up in three years," he said.

"What are you going to do?" I wondered.

"We're moving back to the Midwest."

"And then?"

"We'll find something to do. Maybe travel a little if we get bored."

I kept running into people taking early retirement. Getting out with a pension as young as fifty-five. Some had new jobs lined up. Others were at loose ends, not quite knowing what to do with their new freedom.

One day I told a soon-to-be-retired neighbor that I was thinking of writing a book on life changes, "for people stuck in a dead-end job, for guys out of work, for the newly widowed, for those struck by a crippling adversity, for people like yourself, who are nearing retirement."

His face lit up. "That's a book I want to read!"

The book is done. Some friends may find themselves in the book. The stories are about real people caught in various predicaments and facing new challenges, asking the question of what to do with the rest of their lives. In many cases I've changed names and events and moved locations and times around to disguise identities. Some stories are composites of two or three people, all struggling with the same problem. I've tried not to embarrass anyone. First names only are used for persons who do not wish to be identified. Complete names indicate actual persons.

I have shared much of my own experience in this book. Perhaps it will help to know that the author has faced the same question as the others he has met along this journey.

One final note for this introductory chapter: When considering whether an idea is worthy of a book and is publishable, I always ask two questions:

First: "Who cares?" Who is interested in what I might have to say on this subject? Who wants to know? This is basically a marketing question, which a publisher must ask before signing an author to a contract.

Second: "Who will it help?" Many books, while of intense interest to sizable audiences, are not very helpful. Some are actually destructive, especially to readers with tender minds. As a Christian, I cannot in good conscience write a book just because it bears the mark of a potential best-seller. I must believe that the book will be helpful, encouraging, and challenging—that it will stir readers to take new steps of faith and action and find life more worth living than when they began.

For me, this effort answers both questions affirmatively. I hope that after finishing the book you will agree.

Bogged Down at Forty or Fifty

On February 5, 1947, Adlai Stevenson wrote in his diary, "Am forty-seven today.... What's the matter? Have everything. Wife, children, money, success."

At thirty-eight Brigitte Bardot told an interviewer: "I'm sick of everything.... I detest people. I am allergic to humanity. I no longer see anyone, and I never go out. I have created my own world around me just the way I want it to be—the way it was when I was a child."

A friend of mine in Connecticut, who recently confided that he saw no future in his job, may be more typical. "I'm in the prime of physical life," Jerry said, "but management thinks I'm over the hill. They've given a younger man my position and put me under him. There's no challenge and excitement anymore. I'd quit in a minute if I thought I could get another job paying as much. But with two kids in college and my aged mother to support, I can't afford to take risks. I guess I'm stuck here until retirement."

Sarah, a disheartened housewife, put it differently: "My last child left for college six months ago. I've cleaned and polished and attended club meetings until I'm bored stiff. My husband travels through the week. He comes home on Saturday night and is too tired to go out. Most times I have to get up and go to church by myself. I'd like to get out of this house and get a job. Do something. Anything to make my life worth something. But who would want a high school dropout?"

Professor Edward Hallberg of California State University thinks people like these are caught by the "metapause syndrome." Metapause, says Dr. Hallberg, is a change and pause in one's life when one stops to think about his identity, meaning, and direction. A time in midlife when you are asking: "Who am I? Why am I here? What am I doing? Where am I going? What is the meaning of it all?" A time when you see more sand in the bottom of the hourglass than there is in the top. A time when you think the best years of your life are behind you and the future looks blah. A time when the biblical philosopher may echo your sentiments completely: "Therefore I hated life; because the work that is wrought under the sun is grievous unto me: for all is vanity and vexation of spirit" (Ecclesiastes 2:17).

The more popular label is "midlife crisis," often used of middle-aged males floundering in job and marriage. My fiftyish friend, Dr. Warren Wiersbe, says the much-talked-about midlife crisis is all "humbug," so far as he is concerned. He hasn't experienced it in his life. Middle, age, he writes in *Christianity Today* (May 21, 1982) "is just another stage in a grand and glorious life that has been planned for us by a loving Father."

A much-bandied-about related term is "burnout." According to the experts, burnout can happen to anyone at any time, but usually occurs in midlife. Dr. Herbert J. Freudenberger defines burnout in his book by that name (published by Anchor Press) as "a state of fatigue or frustration brought about by devotion to a cause, way of life, or relationship that failed to produce the expected reward." Ministers, doctors, nurses, social workers, and other people who serve may suffer burnout. So can driven corporate executives, as well as housewives who try to be "Wonder Woman," juggling family and career.

Don't forget woman's "misery," menopause. Technically, menopause marks the end of menstruation and the close of a woman's reproductive cycle at about age forty-eight. Actually, menopause has become a catchall diagnosis for any middle-aged woman's miseries. Some authorities say men enter the menopause stage when they begin stewing over declining sexual powers and asking, "Am I becoming less of a man?" Such a situation, they say, is an affair waiting to happen.

Many women will admit to menopause problems, with some blaming it for whatever ails them at the moment. I've never known a man, however, to blame menopause for his problems. (I do know some department heads in a company who call their president's frequent interoffice notes, "Bill's memo-pause.")

In fairness to females, the best medical evidence says menopause affects only a woman's ability to bear more children. Further physical deterioration need not take place. Many doctors say a woman's enjoyment of sex may even increase after menopause.

Whatever the cause, many of us, male and female, do have problems and ponderings in middle-age. Maybe we are not as severe or tortured as Dante, who plunged into "a dark wood" in "the middle of the road of life." Or as Lord Byron, who called his middle years that "horrid equinox, that hateful section...." The doleful poet Bryon reflected on his birthday:

> *On life's road so dim and dirty*
> *I have dragged to three and thirty.*
> *What have these years left for me?*
> *Nothing—except thirty-three.*

Reflection on the past, the weighing of accomplishments, peering into what appears to be a monotonous, dismal future, can be both emotionally oppressive and physically wrenching. Emotional depression, which tends to color everything with a dark lens, is typically marred by loss of vitality, purposelessness, and boredom. At the same time, a negative emotional change may be affected by other factors, real and imagined, which often occur during middle age.

You sense that mortality is closing in. You think your sun has passed its zenith and is fast sinking toward a clouded horizon.

As a child of six you could hardly imagine being forty or fifty. At fifteen, thirty was old. At twenty, forty-five was too distant to think about. Even at thirty, you scarcely gave a fleeting thought to the fact that your life was probably two-fifths over. Not until you passed forty did you begin to think much about the rest of your life and consider that the options which once seemed so limitless were closing fast.

We men make jokes about how women hide their age, perhaps to cover up our fear of getting old. We say that the longest ten years of a woman's life are between thirty-nine and forty, and before truth-in-mileage laws were passed:

> *Asking a woman her age*
> *Is like buying a secondhand car*
> *The odometer's been set back*
> *But you can't tell how far.*

The other day I saw a gleaming, pink eighteen-wheeler rolling down the interstate. Mary Kay Cosmetics. Tons of chemicals on their way to make women look younger. Then I laughed as I thought of the aids men use. Really, we men are just as vain about our appearance, if not more so.

The fight against fading beauty and youth has churned up multimillion dollar industries. Count the number of TV commercials you see tonight on how to look younger. Cosmetics, beauty treatments, diets, styling, hair dyes, and designer clothes are to make us look better and younger.

You don't care? How do you feel when someone

learns your age and remarks, "I never would have guessed you were that old." Let's admit it. We all want to stay young. That's why young-looking models are predominantly used in commercials and advertisements.

Cosmetics can only change superficial perceptions of how you look. Regardless of how many people say you are looking younger every day, the brutal truth is evident every morning when you wake up and look into a mirror. You *know* that you are getting older.

There are two levels of knowing, one gradual, the other sudden. You're making more trips to the dentist. Changing your glasses more often. Seeing deeper wrinkles in the morning. You don't enjoy staying up as late as you once did. An old classmate, whom you haven't seen in years, suddenly appears and looks "old." You go back for homecoming and the college students look like junior highs. The new "kid" in the office turns out to be thirty-two.

The second level is more painful and for some can be catastrophic. One day a sudden change in relationships, circumstances, or health brings reality crashing down. Your last child is married. You're passed over for a coveted promotion that you thought was "wrapped up." Your doctor writes a prescription for blood pressure pills. You've been aging all your life and lately the signs have become more evident. But it is the *event* that triggers the fear that will not go away. A little "voice" keeps repeating, "Hey, you're no longer young, so quit pretending!"

My "signs" were coming long before I would accept that fact. My oldest daughter got married and had her first child. My youngest entered high school. An eye checkup indicated that I needed glasses for driving; bifocals in a few more years, the optometrist said. My waist began making haste. My parents retired. An uncle died, then an aunt. And what were those white hairs doing around my temples? I kept galloping ahead on the

LIFE CHANGES

imaginary steed of youth. Nothing really fazed me until the firecracker popped in my ear. Suddenly, at forty-seven, I realized I was mortal after all.

This "moment" of truth inevitably arrives. The more you postpone or deny it, the greater may be your fall.

Bill is the long-time vice president of a manufacturing company in Kentucky. He's intelligent, good-looking, and was in ruddy health until a couple of years ago. Bill breezed into his early fifties, dying his hair, pushing fourteen-hour days, pounding the golf course on Saturday with business contacts. Bill was so busy with job, club, and sports activities that he brushed aside any internal whispers that he was getting old. How could he get old when he had a goal to reach—becoming president of his company?

Ten years before, upon joining the firm, he had been promised by the board chairman, "Bill, you'll be president when I step down and our present president becomes chairman." Assurances kept coming that this would be the case. The chairman retired right on schedule. The president moved up. The next announcement, Bill expected, would be for him.

It didn't happen that way. The administrative committee recommended a younger man from out of town. He was thirty-eight. Thirteen years younger than Bill. Bill was dumbfounded when he got the news. Crushed. Angry and hurt, he confronted the retired chairman. "Bill," the silver-haired man assured, "you're indispensable. But we couldn't pass up this man."

Bill stormed out of the restaurant where they had met for lunch. The ladder had been pulled out from under him. He jumped in his car and drove. And drove. All around the city and back again. He felt tired and old, over the hill, trapped at the end of the road. No matter that thousands of men would love to be in his shoes—Bill felt his life was over.

The defeat cast a pall on Bill. He went through the motions of doing his job, quit golf (he couldn't bear to face business friends), stopped shaving on Saturday, crept around the house like an ancient, and found excuses not to attend church. Although he hadn't voiced the words, he had decided just to mark time until he could take retirement at fifty-nine.

Enter Twila, whom Bill happened to sit next to at a trade show banquet. Half his age, she paid attention to him and made him feel younger. Unfortunately, Bill's wife had been no help at all in his crisis. "Why get all upset?" had been her response to his failure to get the presidency. "You make a good salary."

Bill kept finding "business" reasons to call Twila. He set up a "business" lunch with her the next time he was in her city. The business stretched into dinner. They took in a movie. She invited him up to her apartment for coffee (Bill didn't drink). She suggested that he stay the night on her couch and take the early flight home. Bill declined awkwardly and left to catch the night flight.

Unhappily for Bill, his wife found Twila's name and phone number on the jacket of a plane ticket. When she questioned him, he stammered that Twila was only a business acquaintance. After he left for the office she called the number. Twila admitted that they had attended a movie together and he had come up to her apartment.

The wife's fears became exaggerated. When Bill got home, she accused him of sleeping with Twila. No denial could convince her otherwise.

Bill is still marking time at the office. He and his wife are just going through the motions of living together. They tried counseling without success. Bill no longer calls Twila, but there's no spark left in his life. He seldom goes anywhere on the weekend.

Jerry, my friend in Connecticut who suffered a similar job setback, is over the hump of his crisis. He had a tough time for awhile. At the time of his demotion, his hair was still pepper and salt. When I saw him six months later, his head was crowned with white.

The last time I saw Jerry, his hair may have been frosty, but in spirit he was his old self. "I've adjusted," he said. "I don't expect to go any further up the career ladder. I've even come to like my young boss. It helps when he asks my advice and tells me how essential I am to the company. I can see why they hired him. I was getting a little stale. With his vigor and new ideas and my experience, I think we can both really move ahead.

"I've actually come to like having less responsibility," Jerry continued. "I'm doing more in our church. I don't travel so much, and Helen likes that. We're bowling *together* for the first time in years and we're planning a trip *together*. Since my job isn't so all-consuming, she's come to mean a lot more to me."

The rest of Jerry's life looks much more promising than Bill's. Short of a sharp turnaround, Bill will know little joy. Children and grandchildren will keep him from divorce court. He'll be in a stalemate, at least until retirement. Unless he changes, the outlook doesn't look good after that.

There are three big differences in the way Jerry and Bill responded to crisis. Jerry accepted his job situation as it was. Bill wouldn't. Jerry moved some of his energies to more rewarding activities with his wife. Bill continued to sulk. The biggest difference is in their spiritual response. Both are professing Christians. Yet Bill sought no help from his church. He acted as if God were his enemy. Jerry responded positively and continues to grow in faith. He's found Psalm 55:22 to be especially meaningful: "Cast thy burden upon the Lord, and he shall sustain thee."

Women are not necessarily immune to these problems. Although the corporate jungle is still largely a man's haunt, women are coming on fast. As more women take on careers, job-related midlife crises will become more equally divided among the sexes.

Woman's role today in these changing times is about as clear as the proverbial mud. The poor female who tries to heed all of the voices shouting at her will end up not knowing who she is. My grandmothers heard only one voice: marry, have children, and wait on your husband. One had six kids and the other thirteen. My mother taught school a few years before answering love and society's call. She had eight, of which I am the eldest.

Fewer women now see marriage and children as essential to happiness. More than twice as many women (about 45 percent) now hold full-time jobs than did ten years before. Forty-five percent of married mothers with children under six now work outside the home. Many who swallowed the propaganda that they could find fulfillment only in a career are having painful second thoughts. Some are publicly admitting that great damage has been done by extreme feminists. Some are reacting to their declining fertility by desperately trying to have children before the door closes.

Still other women find they must work outside the home by necessity. Some with unemployed husbands are the only breadwinner in their family. They work at the office all day and come home to another day's laundry, cooking, and childtending. They are asking: "Must I be on this frustrating, fatiguing treadmill for the rest of my life?"

There are no easy solutions here, no quick fixes, no waiting limousine to speed you away from frustrations. If you're committed to a career, then the way out of a boring, unfulfilling job may be more education, of which I will say more later. If you're suffering from blatant sex or racial discrimination and being denied a deserved promotion, then you may have to take legal action to secure your rights. If you want children and it isn't too late, you may have to sacrifice career aspirations. If you try to have it both ways, both you and your family may suffer. You'll have to decide and stick to your decision.

If you're killing yourself working for family and employer, something must eventually give. If you have a husband who isn't doing his fair share, you may feel like going on strike and walking a picket line outside your home. Some wives did that in Rhode Island recently. I suspect they did grave damage to their marriages.

Have you considered how much it's costing you to work outside the home? Clothes, carfare, lunches, etc. Add to this the amounts by which you have raised your life style since you started to work. You might find that you can afford to get out of the giddy whirl and concentrate on a higher calling.

Women who give themselves fully to motherhood and family find themselves in a different quandary when their children no longer need them. The last fledgling departs for college, marries, and leaves the nest. The husband has his work. The wife may have only a house, and maybe some pets to mother.

For awhile she may luxuriate in the rest. "The first Monday morning after my Joy went off to college," Phyllis recalled, "I sat down with a cup of coffee and a novel that I'd been trying to finish. Joe had already left for work. There was no one else in the house, except the dog and cat. I didn't have to drag Joy out of bed. It seemed like heaven. I finished that book and a couple of others. I cleaned and dusted and went shopping. I caught up on garden club responsibilities and did a lot of telephoning. After a few months of this, with no real goal before me, I found myself sleeping longer, watching the soaps two and three hours a day, and just muddling through the day until Joe came home. Even then, I didn't have much to say. I could see how bored he was when I kept rattling on. Finally, after one evening of insipid togetherness, Joe told me bluntly: 'You need to get out and do something else with your life.' I didn't appreciate what he said, but I knew he was right. I frittered around a few more days, then went downtown to look for a job."

Sociologist Ruth Jacobs, who went back to school for a graduate degree during midlife, calls women like Phyllis "nurturers." Their prime identity, Dr. Jacobs says in her book *Life After Youth* (Beacon Press), has been in giving to others food, love, and service. As a nurturer you find house chores insufficiently fulfilling. How many times can you wax the kitchen floor? You nag at your husband for being away too often and too late. You drown him with chatter and smother him with affection when he is home—and only cause him to stay away more.

With your former objects of affection absent, you are likely to become preoccupied with yourself without realizing how self-centered you are becoming. You may keep trying new hairdos and beauty potions, trying to hold your man's affection. Failing this, you may try to escape your discontent and unhappiness by spending endless hours with soap operas and drug store novels. At worst, you may start using alcohol or other drugs just to get through the day.

My friends Doris and George married just out of high school. They moved from a rural area to an eastern city and had two beautiful children. George, a tall blond Nordic type, had ambitions beyond his carpenter's trade and started a construction business on the side.

George's business grew into a multimillion-dollar operation. The family moved into a posh subdivision. The kids went to good schools and each got the car of his or her choice at sixteen. By this age both kids had stopped attending Sunday school.

Doris was a beautiful, willowy blonde whom George enjoyed showing off. But as the house and children took up more of her time, she and George went

LIFE CHANGES

out less often. The kids always came first with her. She served as a room mother, president of the PTA, and did all the social things associated with children and school in a suburban neighborhood. Meanwhile George's business kept expanding, and he took up tennis.

After the children left, Doris transferred her energies to house and garden. She began having headaches and was usually sleepless until George came home, usually at a late hour. The doctor told her she was physically OK, and just needed to get out of the house more. She joined a health club. That helped for awhile, but soon the headaches and the sleeplessness returned. The doctor gave her a prescription for a few weeks of sleeping pills. When she asked him for more, he refused. She found a more obliging doctor.

When one of the kids came home for a visit, she cooked lavish dinners. When she could not see them she talked to them almost daily on the phone.

She was now sleeping late, leaving George to get his breakfast downtown. When he did come home early, he would find her in a daze. Finally he called her doctor and demanded to know what she was on. When the doctor gave only vague answers, George confronted Doris. She broke down and admitted that she had a drug problem. "It's only because I'm bored," she sobbed. "The kids are gone. I never see you. I'm sick of doing nothing with my life."

They made some resolutions which went unkept. The last I heard from relatives, Doris was spacier than ever, while George was spending most nights with a girlfriend he had met on the tennis court. He wants a divorce, but not at the price Doris and her lawyer demand. He is drinking heavily. His children know about the girlfriend and refuse to talk to him or let him see his grandchildren.

I see no hope for Doris and George until they are willing to repent (to use an old-fashioned, but still up-to-date biblical word), seek help from God and Christian counselors, and start a new spiritual commitment together. Perhaps then Doris will find something meaningful to do with the rest of her life and George will renew his marriage vows.

Doris and George's problems didn't come in one day. One thing led to another. George might have paid more attention to what was happening at home and shared more in the activities of their children. Doris might have prepared herself for the time when her children would leave.

I know another woman with a much brighter story. When she and her husband were married, they made three priorities: God first, family second, and outside work third. She had to work—a financial necessity—for a couple of years after their first child was born. When her husband, a writer, began earning more money, she came home and concentrated on being a full-time mother and wife. Yet she still found time to keep pace with her husband's intellectual interests. She read at least one book a week and took an occasional adult education course.

When the last of her three daughters entered school, she began free-lance writing. She had been feeding her husband suggestions for years. Now she started putting her ideas to work under her own name and began building a reputation. But when her oldest child arrived home from school, she left her typewriter and became a mother for the rest of the day. In turning down extra writing assignments, she would say: "My girls are still my *primary responsibility*. There'll be more time for writing when they don't need me so much."

Often this meant she could not accompany her husband on trips. When she got an assignment that called for travel, he stayed home with the kids. Together, they planned their work so as to take the children with them on summer research excursions. This way, they spent two summers in Mexico and one in Peru—trips the girls will never forget.

The woman I've been talking about is my wife, Marti. Two of our girls, Cyndi and Cheri, are now married and live near us. Celia finishes college and nurse's training this year. It isn't necessary for Marti to be at their every beck and call. Tomorrow she will leave for a six-week research jaunt to jungled Mindanao in the Philippines. She does not suffer from the "empty nest" syndrome. My capable, conscientious, foresightful wife knows what she will do with the rest of her life.

Marti's case is probably atypical. She frequently says there's "nothing normal" in the life of a writer. She says I helped her develop self-confidence as a writer, since she never had a college course in journalism. She was always a self-assured person, though she told me more than once, "Your expectations are too high for me on this project." I always reply, "I'd rather expect too much of you than too little." I stand by that principle. I've seen too many husbands depreciate their wives' abilities outside the home.

Mary Kay Ash, the cosmetics "queen," has helped thousands of women bridge the fearful gap between home and career. Mary Kay says women seeking employment in midlife typically lack self-confidence. "The job of our sales supervisors," she adds, "is to help our women representatives believe they *can* do *something* with the rest of their lives."

Dr. Jacobs says the woman who has been occupied with home duties since marriage often assumes falsely that she has no useful talents outside the house. Dr. Jacobs, who has counseled hundreds of middle-aged women trying to find their niche, declares: "Homemakers often have great organizational, technical, and managerial ability." How silly, she argues, for a woman who's been running a house and managing children for twenty years to think that she has no job experience.

A long-time friend of ours, Katy, was left a widow at twenty-one with only a high school diploma and two children to support. She worked as a secretary for a few years, married her boss, had another child, and turned back to full-time homemaking.

Her third child entered high school just as Katy turned forty. Her husband had a good job. She did not have to work. Yet she felt unfulfilled, especially when her husband was gone on long business trips.

Katy had never sold anything before. But when a woman friend suggested she might do well in real estate, she took the training and passed the test for a state license. She chalked up a million dollars in sales her first year, a rare accomplishment for a beginner. Katy's husband, a salesman, takes her success in stride. "I taught her everything she knows," he jokes. "Yeah," she replies, "and I've taught him a few things, too."

Having worked as a secretary during young widowhood helped Katy believe she could make it outside a second time. If you worked before marriage or before the birth of your child, you will probably have more self-confidence in looking for a job after forty. If you've been a secretary or nurse, you're almost guaranteed a place in today's job market. Whatever your circumstances, you will be most likely to have a smooth transition if you begin preparing now. The woman who waits until the nest is empty to make plans for the rest of her life is almost guaranteed a rough adjustment.

Perhaps you could get a part-time job when you see your household tasks diminishing. The trick is in being able to control your outside hours while your children still need you.

Another option is volunteering. A number of our friends enjoy helping in church and community activities while their children are still in high school. Later they may go to work full time. Whether you work part time for remuneration or in a volunteer capacity, you will be preparing yourself for the time when the children leave home.

A third option for men or women is additional education. If you don't think you'll need a degree, then go "smorgasbord" and pick the courses which appeal to you most. If you're a woman, look for courses which will prepare you for life after the children have departed.

If you haven't been on a college campus lately, you'll be in for a pleasant surprise. Most of the over-forty people you see carrying books will not be professors, but students. Not only are mamas and papas going back to college, but grandparents too. They're going to learn, train for new careers, retool, or just broaden their understanding.

The traditional college or university that cannot adjust may not survive many more years. Demographics show a diminishing number of youth reaching the eighteen-to-twenty-one-year traditional college age during the next few years. Colleges must look for older persons to make up for the gap, and keep the tenured professors teaching. But that isn't the only reason astute admissions people are going after the more mature. They know that mental powers broaden with age. Older students may not be able to think as fast, but they have the advantage of accumulated experiences and a better ability to see the big picture.

Some of these older students you now see on campus are also employed. Their employers are footing part or all of the education bill. By getting to know these older, working students, you'll be making valuable contacts for the time when you're ready to enter the job market.

If you don't have an employer or a spouse with enough income to cover educational expense, don't be dismayed. Visit the financial aid office and inquire about scholarships and loans. You'll have the same chance as the younger set. Age discrimination is strictly illegal, as every administrator now knows.

Contrary to what many think, aid is still available. You can probably get a guaranteed student loan if you can show financial need. Loan restrictions apply mostly to people with incomes of $30,000 and above.

A new magazine, *50-plus*, which ought to be on your reading list (even if you're only forty) recently published an "Off to College" report for the mature set (September 1982, pp. 20-29).* Here are some examples of educational opportunities:

The University of San Francisco offers the College of Professional Studies for special needs of middle-aged and older persons. One fourth of the 1,800 adults enrolled are over fifty. Credits are given for life and work experience. Everyone enters with at least one year of college.

The University of Albuquerque (New Mexico) has 475 adults enrolled in its College of Nontraditional Studies. Says Associate Dean William F. Wagner:

> Adults learn differently from people coming straight out of high school. Adults are more interested in integrating the material into some kind of whole. Also, relevance is more important to adults: "How does what I'm learning fit into my world? [they ask]."

George Washington University in Washington, D.C., offers interesting certificate programs for college graduates wanting to acquire practical job skills in such professions as law, publishing, fund-raising, landscape design, and computer science. (Don't make the mistake of

---

*Published by Retirement Living Publishing co., 850 Third Ave., New York, NY 10022. $15.00 annual subscription.

assuming that your twenty-year-old bachelor's degree qualifies you for *today's* job market.)

You can easily get more information on schools in your area by checking catalogues in your municipal library or visiting the schools close by.

Higher education opportunities are for all types of adults in all kinds of circumstances. Male, female, employed, self-employed, unemployed, homemaker, parent, grandparent, whoever, whatever. Especially for adults who want to get a new jump and fresh insights into what they really want to do for the rest of their life.

Like Harold Mitzelfelt who had a secret desire to become a doctor. Harold was forty-six and head of the music department at a Massachusetts college when he enrolled for night classes in a pre-med program. He accumulated enough credits and high enough grades to gain admittance to the University of Tennessee Medical School. He resigned from his job, dug into savings, moved south, and took a part-time post as a church choir director. His wife, supporting him fully in the career change, gave piano lessons to supplement his income.

Four years later he got his M.D.

I heard of another fellow of forty who expressed a longing to become a doctor. "But it'll take me at least four years and I'll be forty-four when I start my internship," he lamented.

"Granted," a friend responded, "but have you considered that you'll be the same age in four more years, whether you take the medical course or not?"

He applied and was admitted.

One evening, a few weeks after my ear injury catapulted me into a painful midlife examination, I was browsing in our metro library. For years I had toyed with the idea of getting a Ph.D. in mass communications, specializing in broadcasting and journalism—two fields in which I had practical experience. I had made four negative assumptions: One, my undergraduate work was not in communications and I could not be admitted to grad school. Two, my grades during my first two years of college were horrible, mostly Cs and Ds and a couple of Fs. (After I became a Christian my grades picked up dramatically!) Three, the only graduate schools in mass communications were hundreds of miles away. I didn't want to uproot my family, even if the move was affordable. Fourth, I couldn't attend graduate school and keep working to pay the bills. I was also at an age at which I thought my sanity might be questioned if I returned to school.

Just out of curiosity, I thumbed through the catalog of the University of Tennessee at Knoxville, and discovered that UT offered a Ph.D. in mass communications. UT was only one hundred miles up the interstate. Tuition was cheap for in-state residents.

Feeling brave and foolhardy, I wrote and requested an interview. Dean Donald Hileman of the College of Communications invited me up and took me to lunch. He suggested I make application, but not be disappointed if I was rejected. "Most of our students are a little younger than you," he said kindly.

I sent my academic transcripts. I explained why my grades were so poor during my first two years in college. I sent a couple of books and a few articles I had written. Dean Hileman and the director of graduate studies were noncommittal. "After you take the Graduate Record Examinations, we'll take your application to the committee," the Dean promised. "That'll be a year from now, because the admittance deadline for this year is already past."

The GRE scared me, even though the date for taking the exam was six months away. I had not been a student for over twenty years. How could I possibly compete with young minds just out of college?

A couple of things helped. I started a running program, increasing to six miles a day. This gave me physical and mental vigor which I had not felt for years. Second, I began reviewing a wide range of subject matter. I dove into *The World Book Encyclopedia*, starting with the "A" volume and reading at least thirty minutes each day. Then one happy day my collegiate daughter brought home a GRE review book from the university bookstore. Here were hundreds of examples of the types of questions asked on GRE exams.

I took the test in January and performed slightly above average in the quantitative and analytical divisions, and way above (in the eighty-fourth percentile) in verbal scores. Yet I still felt my chances were no better than one in ten, since only about five doctoral students in mass communications were being admitted by UT each year.

Finally in May the notification came. No eighteen-year-old freshman ever opened a letter with greater anxiety. There it was: "You have been admitted as a doctoral student." I felt like dancing on the kitchen table.

I discovered that a number of doctoral students actually were older than I. One man had a stroke during graduate study and returned to finish his dissertation! One woman, a retired nurse, was past sixty-five and getting her doctorate in education "so I can be better prepared to supervise literacy workers."

The first weeks were the hardest. Arriving Sunday evening at midnight and sleeping in a lonely room rented from a fellow graduate student. Cold mornings spent trying to find a parking place, then rushing to class. Awkward exchanges with fellow students the age of my children. Long tiresome drives back home. Late night toiling over tedious research papers. Many times I wondered, "Why am I punishing myself? Why am I robbing my family of companionship?" After each questioning, assurance would come that God was with me, that the sacrifice was worth what the graduate degree would mean for the rest of my life. God provided financially, too. Scholarships paid most of my tuition. I continued to receive free-lance assignments. With Marti working full time and me part time, along with a low-interest student loan, we managed to scrape by.

During two particularly tough quarters, I commuted with Betty Cox, a doctoral student in education. Two days a week, I left home at six A.M., picking up Betty a half hour later, and getting home at midnight. Betty, an attractive, thirtyish mother of a four-year-old daughter, told me she had been teaching elementary school. "One day, I asked myself, is this what I want to do for the rest of my life? I said 'No.' With my husband's encouragement, I applied for graduate school."

Betty had a second child during her second year of study. She attended classes right into her ninth month, frightening some of her professors. Marti suggested that I ought to know how to deliver a baby, should Betty's time come on the highway to Knoxville. Her second daughter was born just after the end of the term. Dr. Betty Cox is now head of a department at Chattanooga State and Technical Community College.

Three years and three months after entering, I mounted the platform to receive my hood and hear the university officials say, "Congratulations, Doctor."

Marti and our three daughters were in the audience. Just as the hood was being slipped over my shoulders, the girls screamed, "Way to go, Dad!" Everybody could hear them. Marti told the woman sitting next to her, "If you think they're loud, you should hear his grandchildren!"

The doctorate, received just a month ago, opened a new vista of opportunities. I'm eternally glad to have made the trip. If I hadn't, I would still be the same age today—fifty-two.

LIFE CHANGES

Whatever your circumstances and your discouragements, please believe that you can make the rest of your life count. You're not finished until you think you are. The best and most fulfilling days of your life can be ahead, if you're willing to start preparing now.

Remember:

Henry Ford was practically broke and unknown at forty. After forty he raised $28,000 to establish the Ford Motor Company and develop the assembly line that brought the world fast mass transportation.

Harry Truman was forty when his haberdashery business failed in Kansas City. Having only a high school education, he turned to politics, was elected county judge, and advanced to the highest office in the United States.

Robert Frost published his first book of poetry at forty, and was not planning to do any more writing until readers read his poems and urged him to do more.

Dwight Eisenhower was stuck in the rank of major for sixteen years, from age thirty to forty-six. He broke out and moved up to be the greatest general of World War II, then was elected President.

Winston Churchill was considered a washed-up politician at forty. Refusing to become a castoff, he became prime minister of England at age sixty-five.

Wallace E. Johnson was stone broke at forty. Determined to do something with the rest of his life, he mortgaged his car for $250, found a man who wanted a house built, and obtained a construction loan from a bank. Earning $181 on his first house, he built another the same way. Then another and another until he was building hundreds. Later he joined up with Kemmons Wilson, who had built the first "Holiday Inn." By standardizing designs and franchising inns to builders, they established the largest chain of motels in the world.

Walter Knott and his wife couldn't make enough from farming in the California desert to support their four kids. They moved to a more fertile area in Buena Park and tried raising boysenberries. They sold the berries at a roadside stand.

Mrs. Knott added berry pies, biscuits, and chicken dinners to their offerings. To keep customers entertained, the Knotts set up glass beehives, candy-making exhibits, and talking myna birds. They kept adding variety until Knott's Berry Farm became a worldwide attraction.

Plenty of other people are known for what they've done after forty or fifty. Look around you. You've probably overlooked some daring acquaintances who have proven that it can be done.

You can do it, and if you're a Christian you're way ahead of the pack. When you received Christ as Savior and Lord, God started something wonderful in your life. He promises to fulfill what he started: Being "confident of this very thing, that He who began a good work in you will perfect it until the day of Christ Jesus" (Philippians 1:6, NASB).

But you must cooperate and allow him to help you grow in obedience and faith. If you've been bogged down in mediocrity and aimlessness, take his hand *now*. Rise up, get on your feet, and get going on the marvelous plan he has for the rest of your life.

3

Out of a Job... or About to Be

Harry is a big, robust, ruddy-faced guy with rippling muscles and a warm, open-faced smile. The friendly scoutmaster, Sunday-school-teacher type with a wife, three kids, first and second mortgages on his house, and utility bills.

I met Harry one sunny April morning in Tucson. I had been booked as a communications consultant for his church, and was scheduled to visit the local TV stations that day. Harry popped into the church office and overheard me asking the secretary for directions around town.

"Let me drive you—I know this town," he offered, after introducing himself. "I have nothing else to do today."

"Sure, glad to have the company," I replied and took him to the car. "You can probably cut the time in half."

Harry headed us out into the rush-hour traffic, past where some elderly folks were pulling out of a trailer park. "Snowbirds," he noted. "They live up North, come down here to winter, then go back in the spring. Must be nice not having to worry about mortgages and kids going to college."

I ventured what I had already suspected: "You're looking for a job?"

"Have been for weeks. That's how I know the town so well. I was laid off last December from the Duval

Mining Company. Reckon the company couldn't beat the foreign competition."

"Arizona is having the same problem as Michigan?"

"Not from the Japanese. Our competition is in Zaire, Peru, and a few other countries. It's cheaper to buy copper overseas and have it shipped here than to buy from the mine where I got laid off."

"Understanding doesn't provide much comfort, I guess."

Harry smiled grimly. "Sure doesn't. What the economists and the politicians say won't pay my mortgage."

"First time you've been laid off?"

"Second. Several years ago I made the list. We had enough to get by and I took it as an opportunity to do something for the Lord. Happened that our church needed a bus driver just then to take the young people to a retreat. I had the time of my life. It was also one of the best times our family ever had."

"Then the mine called you back?"

"Yeah, just as they'd promised. I figured the same thing would happen this time. Last December 14 they tacked a notice on the bulletin board at the mine saying 1,820 of us would be laid off. By the time I got home, Mary had already seen it on the TV news. 'Not to worry,' I said. 'With my seniority I'm bound to be called back.'

"We cut back on our spending, just in case. We bought presents for the kids the day after Christmas and got some super buys. Turned out to be one of our best family Christmases ever.

"By February I was getting a little restless. Then the company announced that 1,400 would be brought back in March on a seniority basis. I knew I was high enough to be included and looked forward to getting back to the old grind. Well, they took only 600 and stopped just above my seniority. That's when I hit the streets looking for another job. Hey, there's channel four."

We parked near the entrance of the NBC affiliate. "Mind if I come with you?" he asked. He hung on to every word as I talked with a producer about an upcoming church feature.

"Any job possibilities?" I wondered when we were back in the car.

"I qualified as a truck driver at one place. They would give me only $3.40 an hour. I couldn't pay two mortgages and buy groceries on that.

"But yesterday I interviewed for driving a city transit bus. The pay is better and the security looks good. I'm to take the psychological test tomorrow. I've got my hopes up."

We made another stop. "What if you don't get the bus driving job?" I asked when we were back in the car.

"Well, I'll just know the Lord has something else. Doesn't the Bible say that God will provide for his people? What's that verse in Philippians, 'My God shall supply all your need...'?"

" 'According to his riches in glory by Christ Jesus,' " I finished.

"I reckon the Lord's unemployment fund is unlimited."

We rode on a few blocks. "If I don't get that job with the city, I sure hope the Lord will do something soon. We may have to let our house go back in a couple of weeks and rent an apartment. That'll be tough on my family. But if we have to do it, we have to do it."

"How old are your kids, Harry?" I asked, thinking it might be better to change the subject.

"One's in grade school. Two in high school. My oldest boy is due to go to college this fall. I had hoped to have some money for his tuition. As things stand, he'll have to work full time, if he can get a job.

"This being unemployed affects everybody in your family," Harry continued. "It hurts not being able to help my boy. I'd always counted on that. A man at forty-four ought to be set in his career and have a little laid by to help his kid get a better education than he had."

Harry was choking up.

"You'll have to forgive me for feeling sorry for myself. Here I am with only a high school diploma and no special skill except to drive a truck and work in a copper mine. I'll tell you something that's been going through my mind. If the Lord gets me a job, any job, so I can take care of my family, I'm going to enroll in night school and retrain for one of the coming industries. You don't think it's too late for me, do you?"

"No, Harry," I said with assurance. "You're going to make it."

"God helping me, I'm going to make it. I've got to. The folks at the church are praying for me. And my family is sticking with me all the way."

That day I learned something about the agony of unemployment from a man of faith. I also learned something about those whose faith is weak or lacking. "Some of my buddies who were laid off with me are spending their evenings in bars," Harry said sadly. "They're drowning their troubles, spending money their families need for groceries."

Harry and other unemployed copper miners in Arizona are among the 10.8 percent of Americans now out of work (the highest number of unemployed workers since the year before Pearl Harbor when it was 14.6 percent). The numbers were much worse in 1933 when more than one in four could not find a job.

If you're in Harry's shoes or about to be, it may not be very encouraging to know that your misery has lots of company. Or to know that we are now in a worldwide recession. In many countries more than 50 percent of the population are without jobs. There are simply not enough jobs to go around for all who need to work. Prospects for the future are not exactly rosy.

Some of us remember the Great Depression. My mother and dad started their family in 1930. We lived in a log cabin sheltered in an Ozark Mountain cove. A thin garden, a few acres of corn on a rocky hillside, a cow, an old mare, a few pigs and chickens, and a hunting dog were about all we had. Our only cash money came from animal hides that brought a quarter apiece. The only industry was a two-man saw mill, five miles down the valley, to which we took our shelled corn for grinding. The miller kept a peck from each bushel as his pay.

When hides dropped to a nickel, the government brought in the Works Progress Association, popularly called the WPA. Daddy walked ten miles a day, round trip, to work with pick and shovel for a dollar a day. There was no minimum wage or food stamps. By today's standards we were abysmally poor and deprived. But somehow my parents kept food on the table and had a warm bed for their children at night.

That's why some of us who survived the Great Depression find it hard to empathize with the plight of today's unemployed. We remember how it was back on the farm, where you could hunt meat, raise a garden, have laying chickens, and milk a cow. We forget that few have those privileges today. Almost everything we eat and wear now must come from a store.

Seldom did a week pass during my childhood when uncles and aunts and cousins didn't come visiting. The pallet was always ready to be spread. There was plenty of wood for the fireplace and plenty of places to play. I knew who I was. Until my twelfth birthday I had never heard of a couple getting divorced. Families aren't the same today.

We didn't have television then. We couldn't see

in full color what we lacked. College was for the faraway rich. I was the first among sixty-eight-plus cousins to complete high school and enroll in college.

And hardly anybody worried about what to do in life. What else could anybody do but farm?

That simple life is gone forever. By today's living standards, the "good ole days" were very bad. We just didn't know how bad they were.

Now we have a minimum wage, food stamps, and unemployment compensation. But the minimum wage is meaningless to people out of work. Unemployment benefits run out, even programs that pay 90 percent of the working wage, as many auto workers have learned.

Food stamps are not the easy gravy which some affluent Americans imagine. Ernest Bertoldo, who was laid off along with Harry, has a wife and three kids. He got unemployment benefits from the mining company for three months. This left him with $95 a week in state unemployment compensation. He thought he might still make it with food stamps. But his application was denied. "You have equity in a truck that exceeds the $1,500 limit on personal property established for stamps," he was told. "Man, I owe more than my equity on the truck," he protested. "I need the truck to find a job and then get work," he said. "Sorry, this is the rule," the clerk responded.

Unemployment is unevenly divided among groups. More blue-collar workers than white-collars are out of work, more blacks than whites, more among high school graduates than college graduates, and more in their fifties than in their thirties and forties. Unemployment is also higher in some states and cities. And occupations such as autos and steel are hit harder than others.

Low percentages mean nothing if you're in the low group and out of work. There are thousands with college degrees out of work. Some with doctor's and master's degrees can't get anything. A service station owner told an educator who applied, "I can't take a risk on you. You'd quit in a minute if something opened in your field." A museum manager told a young college graduate in art applying for a custodian's job, "You're overqualified." Small comfort.

Here was my old friend Bert, whom I introduced in chapter one, jobless and sinking deeper and deeper into debt every day. One day, several months after he lost his job, I happened to be in his town on business. I called him from my motel and asked how things were going. "Very bad," he said. "I'd invite you over, but you'd freeze. Our heat has been cut off."

Bert is well educated and well traveled, the kind you meet at the country club. In better times he and I had agreed that the long-term unemployed are mostly deadbeats sponging off taxpayers by taking welfare and food stamps—people who would run from a job if it were offered. We had always said, "Anybody who wants a job can get one. Just look at all the ads in the paper." Things had changed. We had changed.

"I don't enjoy going to church anymore," Bert said. "A guy asks, 'How are you?' What am I to say? 'I'm out of work. My heat's been cut off. I can't buy clothes for the kids.' Maybe I should say that, but I don't. Our church is so big and the people so well off, that I doubt if anybody would understand."

Bert was obviously depressed. "Let me take you to dinner," I suggested.

"Well, uh-" I could read the hesitancy in his voice. Bert was proud. He didn't want charity, not even from a friend.

"Bring Ruby," I added. "We'll talk about old times, better times." He was still hesitating. "Look, pal, come on," I insisted. "You may have to take me to dinner someday."

They drove up in an old heap a few minutes

later. "It's borrowed," Bert explained. "Our Buick was repossessed." Thankfully the lights were soft and low in the restaurant. I'm sure they didn't want me to see the lines in their haggard faces.

Unemployment can be a terribly traumatic experience. Being out of a job can shatter your self-esteem. Especially when others around you have good jobs.

"You get to thinking something may be wrong with you," Bert said.

Our work tells the world what we can do. Being an employed carpenter, accountant, teacher, or machinist makes us somebody in the eyes of many people. So an unemployed father was crushed at overhearing his son and another little boy talking. "My daddy's a plumber and he's strong," the young visitor bragged. To this the jobless man's son replied, "My daddy's a nothing but he's stronger."

Dr. James Gallagher, chairman of the career consulting firm in New York City that bears his name, says unemployment hits a super-ambitious person hardest because he "invests so much identity in his job title . . . his first question is, 'If I'm not vice president of marketing for the XYZ Comapny, who am I?' His next question is, 'How am I going to survive?' " He is not talking about his physical life, Dr. Gallagher says, "but the quality of the life he's built up. His third question is: 'How do I face my family? Friends? Business colleagues?' Losing a job is a terrible blow to the ego."

Albert Bragg, a jobless thirty-three-year-old West Virginian, told a Congressional hearing on unemployment of how he had actually put a .30-30 rifle to his head and pulled the trigger. "I guess I moved my head," he said. "I'm sorry for doing it. I just couldn't take the pressure. I was just scared." He began crying, then apologized. "I'm sorry," he sobbed. "I was proud to be a steelworker."

Ida Hines, an unemployed teacher from Baltimore, testified at the same hearing. She described her problems as the head of a household of four children, one with multiple sclerosis. She conceded her anger: "I went through the system. I worked. Now I am a degreed person out of a job. It's very depressing. I don't enjoy being unemployed. When you are out of a job, you are looked at as being shiftless no matter how much education you have. You feel less than a person."

Being out of work can sorely test your family relationships. I know a family in which the wife has a good job and the husband only works part time mowing lawns. Both are college graduates. He spends a lot of time baby-sitting, since they cannot afford a sitter. He is expected to cook some of the meals. Perhaps this should not affect him, but it does. He can hardly escape the tradition of his family and peers in which the husband is expected to be the main breadwinner. The marriage of this couple is showing cracks.

A man or woman can become desperate. Tony Garza's aerial mapping business, which he had operated successfully for twenty-seven years, folded in Ohio after government contracts dried up. Unable to find other work in Ohio, Tony and his wife Kay migrated to San Antonio and looked for work. A month later, both were found fatally shot in the front seat of their car. Tony left bankruptcy papers, an empty wallet, a rifle, and a suicide note that said: "I have gone as far as I can with our lives. Kay and I are hard-working people that have been almost reduced to begging."

Their deaths were ruled murder and suicide. Neighbors who had known them in Ohio were aghast. "Tony just wasn't the type," said one. "He seemed to be happy. Nothing seemed to bother him."

Not every unemployed person goes this far. Certainly not those who are only recently out of work. But those who have been jobless for months confide to counselors and friends of unprecedented financial pressure, loss of self-esteem, and family strain. One of my long-time jobless friends told me, "Lately I've been thinking of a way to kill myself that will permit my wife to collect on my insurance." This man is a professing Christian, an active worker in his church.

A fellow I know in Houston—where there are supposed to be lots of jobs—was out of work for several months and had to take a second mortgage on his house. Unexpected medical bills drove him deeper into debt. He got a new job, but it did not pay enough to stave off financial disaster. "I've been served notice of foreclosure," he said. "I can survive, but I'm not sure about Jane. During all the time I was off, the house was her one security. She kept saying, 'We must not lose the house.' Now that it looks as if we will lose it, I'm afraid she will go over the wall."

Hopefully, you're not this bad off. Maybe you aren't unemployed—yet. But you know your job is shaky. You've seen that your company's sales are way down. The economic forecast for your industry is very poor. There's a rumor out that headquarters in New York is going to close a sister plant in another state next week, and that your plant may be next.

If you have advance knowledge, don't wait for the axe to fall before you get started on a new plan. It's always easier to find other work while you're still working. You have a better image value to prospective employers. You have more bargaining leverage when you aren't perceived as being desperate. And you're better equipped psychologically and financially. So don't wait for the inevitable. Be like the ant who said to his friend after the golfer had sliced off most of their hill in three bad swings: "If we're going to make it, we'd better get on the ball!" Get on the ball and get moving.

If you've received final notice or have just collected your last paycheck, you may not be in a healthy emotional state. Still you must make yourself do certain necessities before trying to get your act together. After you've taken care of the paperwork at your old office or plant, go to the unemployment office and file for benefits. Put in your application for food stamps. If this hurts your pride, think of it as getting back a little of your tax money. But do it now, for the wheels of bureaucracy can move maddeningly slow.

Joan, a young mother of two whose company went bankrupt, told me, "We worked day and night to keep the company afloat. We let our paychecks slide for several weeks, hoping that sales might improve. When the owners finally declared bankruptcy, I needed money for groceries, like last month. My back pay wasn't a secured debt. I lost it all. I ran down to the unemployment and food stamp offices, expecting to get help immediately. I almost died when they told me how long it would be. 'How am I going to feed my kids?' I screamed at the woman in the food stamp office. She shrugged and said in a tired monotone, 'Try the Salvation Army.'"

After you've done what you have to do, put in a job application at a couple of places, just for the peace of mind of knowing that your line's in the water. Then take a little time to cool off and formulate a battle plan.

Psychologists say that a suddenly unemployed person is likely to go into shock. "How can this have happened to me?" he asks. "Why must my family have to suffer from crummy management that let the company go under, outrageous union demands that priced us out of the market, stupid government cutbacks that robbed us of new contracts?" Your blood boils every time you think of what happened. You grind your teeth while trying to fix the blame.

You may feel used, betrayed, taken for a ride, discarded, especially if the company kept promising that things would get better and then suddenly announced that disaster had come. You can't sleep. You feel anxious all the time. You snap at your family over the least provocation.

Get out of the house. Go fishing. Go on retreat. Go anywhere to get away from THE PROBLEM for a few hours or days. But don't spend much time alone. Find someone you can talk to with whom you can be natural, someone who is a good listener. But not one of your old work buddies who's in the same pit you are and doesn't know how he will get out.

Remember the old spiritual, "Steal Away." Now is the time to "steal away to Jesus." Maybe you're ashamed to be asking for the Lord's help. When your life was going well, when the money was rolling in, when you were making it yourself, you forgot the Great Sustainer. Don't be embarrassed to go back and take his hand. He's had a billion more like you.

Call it foxhole religion, or whatever. That's the way of our fickle nature. And he knows it. The sin of Adam and everyone else is to stand independent from God. Thankfully, our God is merciful. His phone is never too busy to take your call. His office door is always open. Like the father of the prodigal son, when he sees you coming in sincere repentance, he will have compassion and meet you coming up the walk. "The Lord is nigh unto them that are of a broken heart" (Psalm 34:18).

When you are willing to admit that you are unworthy in his sight, he will make you worthy. He will raise your self-esteem and give you the best identification and security man can know. Then it can be said: "Now you belong to Christ Jesus, and though you were once far away from God, now you have been brought very near to him because of what Jesus Christ has done for you with his blood" (Ephesians 2:13, TLB). You will "know that all that happens to [believers] is working for our good if we love God and are fitting into his plans" (Romans 8:28, TLB).

He promises to meet the needs of his children. Needs, not wants. He never saws us off on a "limb." If he asks us to take risks, he'll follow behind to hold us.

Marti and I have witnessed his faithfulness. Early in our marriage we were serving a little mission church in a poverty-stricken back corner of New Orleans. We were paid from the offerings after other bills were satisfied. For several Sundays our check was never more than a few dollars. We told no one as we watched our cupboard diminishing day by day. One evening after we had given thanks over crackers and soup, one of the deacons arrived with two big bags of groceries.

A couple of years later our income took another sharp downturn. Marti opened the last can. She served the last piece of bread. Nothing more was left to feed our year-old baby, Cyndi. I failed to realize what was happening. After I left to make some pastoral visits, she knelt and simply said, "Lord, we belong to you. We're doing your work. We can miss a meal or two, but Cyndi needs nourishment now."

Three hours later she hopefully went to the mailbox. I had mailed two or three short free-lance articles a couple of weeks before. There was an envelope with a check for eight dollars from the Salvation Army magazine, *War Cry!* We've received much larger amounts from writing in the years since, often just in time to meet a definite need. But no check was ever more treasured.

Most career counselors will probably not tell you this. But as one who has found the Lord faithful, I will. First make your peace *with* him and find your peace *in* him. Transfer to him your heavy burden of low self-confidence, uncertainty, and fear.

After you have prayed, do not sit and wait for

the sparrows to bring you food. Take advantage of whatever means that are available. God provides through all channels. He is Lord of all the earth, including friends, your church, and the social programs of the government.

He also expects you to budget, plan, and use the wisdom which he will give as you have need. Sit down with your spouse and review the family finances. List your absolute necessities and fixed expenses: house payment or rent, car payment, insurance, utilities, food, minimum installment payments, medical bills, church gifts, etc. Add up whatever income you can count on while out of work: your spouse's salary, if working; unemployment insurance; severance pay; investment interest; etc. If you have savings, postpone any withdrawals as long as you can.

If you're out of balance, trim a few dollars off the bill of each creditor and write each one, asking permission to pay the reduced amount. Most will probably go along. Then consider how you might cut back on food (powdered milk for whole milk, for example) and other items considered essential.

If your children are past infancy, let them know what the family *must* do. They will take the cutbacks better than you think. Allow them to pray with you for a job. Keep everyone informed of what is happening.

Suppose you find you still can't make it? Perhaps the creditors won't cooperate. Perhaps the bills are just too many and too widely scattered. Visit a credit counseling agency, not a finance company where you may lose a great deal by consolidating your bills. Your pastor, United Fund agency, or any social worker can tell you where to get help. The credit counselor will divide your funds available for paying bills among your creditors and try to secure their cooperation.

In dire need, ask your pastor if your church has an emergency fund. Most churches do. You may have friends who will help, but you must let them know. When you do seek a loan from a friend or relative, offer to sign a promissory note that pledges you to pay back in specific installments or a lump sum.

A member of my Sunday school class, a major executive in a large company, recalled a time when he was down and out. "I went to see a couple of friends and told them my problem. The first one prayed with me. The second pulled out his checkbook and said, 'How much do you need?' When you're really down, you find out who your friends really are."

What if your creditors are hounding you unmercifully, even though there are laws to prevent extreme harassment? You may have to strap on your parachute, bail out, and take bankruptcy. Around 500 businesses are taking this step every week, along with thousands of individuals. Many are Christians.

Can bankruptcy be a last-ditch provision of God? Sometimes. Bankruptcy is a means established by law for financially ruined persons to survive with the minimum necessities of life.

I know a husky builder, an officer in his church, who was caught by rising interest rates. First, he lost his unsold houses to the bank that had provided the construction financing. Next, he lost his home, forcing his family to rent. With creditors snapping at his heels and his wife's health precarious, he finally filed for bankruptcy. "We just couldn't take any more pressure," he said.

Susan, a forty-five-year-old single woman in Los Angeles, lived on cash advances from her credit cards for months while she was out of work. At $15,000 in debt, she managed to get a part-time job. She had the debt whittled to $12,000 when her landlord slapped her with a big rent hike. This and worries about her health drove her to a bankruptcy lawyer. "I saw that it would take me ten years to get out of debt and I wouldn't have anything saved for my retirement," she said. "What else could I do?"

Chapter Thirteen of the bankruptcy laws allows you to hang onto your property. The court freezes your debts and works out an extended payment plan with those you owe. This is much like credit counseling, except the debtors are told by the court to cooperate.

Chapter Seven, total bankruptcy, calls for your assets above a minimum amount to be sold and the proceeds divided up among your debtors. Your debts are wiped out but you lose your credit rating and cannot take bankruptcy again for six years. You're allowed to retain up to $7,500 equity in a house and $1,200 in a motor vehicle; up to $200 investment in each of several household items; up to $500 worth of jewelry; and up to $750 investment in the tools of your trade. These exemptions are double when a husband and wife file jointly.

We discussed bankruptcy in Sunday school. Everyone agreed that bankruptcy was sometimes unavoidable and not a sin. We divided over a Christian's obligation to pay back debts relieved by the courts.

A young businessman saw a difference between business and personal debts. "All businesses," he said, "allow for a certain debt risk when they loan money or extend credit for goods. A friend usually does not. He may loan you money at great personal sacrifice. I would repay him when able, even if I was not legally bound."

Expense trimming, credit counseling, an emergency loan from Aunt Minnie, bankruptcy, whatever is just bailing water to stay afloat. You've got to make your craft secure. You must get on with finding a job. So we're back to the big question: What are you going to do with the rest of your life?

Survey after survey indicates that most people don't really enjoy their work. Gallup asked a cross-section of American adults twenty-seven years ago: "Do you enjoy your work so much that you have a hard time putting it aside?" Fifty-two percent then said yes. Gallup repeated the question in 1955 and 40 percent said yes. By 1980 the number enjoying their work was down to 34 percent.

Now may be your opportunity to get into something you really enjoy. You're older and your values have changed. Status (and even money if you can afford it) isn't as important as doing something you love, something you believe is making a contribution to humanity. More to the point, maybe now is your opportunity to do what you've felt for many years the Lord wants you to do.

Bill Summers was among the air controllers fired by President Reagan in the government's confrontation with their union. Being out of work after thirteen years of directing air traffic brought Bill face-to-face with a decision he had put off for years.

"The Lord let me know I had run out of excuses," Bill explained. "I told the Lord, 'I'm going to do whatever you want.'"

That was to preach. He enrolled for ministry training at Boyce Bible School Seminary in Louisville, Kentucky. A year later Bill became student pastor of a church in Kentucky and was on his way.

Suppose your skills are unmarketable or the industry in which you long worked is on a steep downgrade. Not long ago I stopped at the office of an industrialist friend in Houston. His paint manufacturing plant is located in the heart of a busy industrial district. "How's the job picture around here?" I asked Dale.

"There's work for those who have the skills in demand," he observed. "But almost all of those coming to us can't qualify for what we need. A lot of them worked on assembly lines up North. They were making fifteen dollars an hour, doing one little task over and over. To work in my plant, they must understand the chemistry of mixing the elements in paints. About all they can get around here, if they're lucky, is a laborer's job, pushing a broom or cleaning up a warehouse for five dollars an hour. Their families can't live on that."

I thought of what Dale had said when I saw a TV feature on Houston's "Tent City" where hundreds of northern immigrants are camping out in the weather while searching for work.

I heard the same story in other states, from Alaska to Florida, while researching this book: "People who don't have the skills we want shouldn't come here."

You'd have to be blind, deaf, and dumb to miss the shout in economic news lately. The western nations are in a new industrial revolution. The economy is cascading into computer technology, electronics, communications, service jobs, and health-related occupations. A couple of months ago I talked to an officer in a company that makes computer software. "We're looking for thirty designers and programmers," he said. "Like *yesterday!*"

Four friends of mine just received their doctorates in mass communications. All have good teaching jobs at prestigious universities. Our daughter Celia will receive her degree in nursing this year. She has already received scores of job solicitations from hospitals.

The other day a blue-ribbon commission of Tennessee businessmen delivered a scorching criticism of administrators in vocational and technical schools. "Many of your courses are not in tune with changing business requirements," a commission member said. He listed twenty-six occupations which are expected to be in highest demand in Tennessee within the next ten years. The top five relate to computer technology.

Retraining may be crucial, if you're laid off from a dying industry. Just be sure you're retooling for a job that will be there when you've finished. The

Tennessee commission referred to above noted that practically all the state's vocational schools offer training in cosmetology, while job opportunities have sharply declined in recent years.

Don't be taken in by a glib admissions counselor who wants only to keep the faculty at his school working. He needs students. Just be sure you need what his school offers.

After Cam and Georgie Miars' business failed, they lost their home. Cam was fifty-one years old. When Cam could not find a job he wanted, they both enrolled in Michigan State University, where their youngest daughter Joan was already studying.

The financial aid office showed them how to finance their study. For the first year, they got Pell Grants ($1,556 each), Guaranteed Student Loans ($2,500 each at 9 percent interest; not repayable until after graduation). and work-study programs. This was enough to cover their on-campus living expenses.

Cam already had enough college credit to qualify as a junior majoring in business, while Georgie entered as a sophomore. She made the dean's list the first semester, while Cam missed it by only a whisker. They're still in school at this writing. They have a tough schedule with morning and afternoon classes, work-study, and internships, plus four hours of study each day. Both are confident of better times ahead.

If you find yourself unemployed in midlife, a traditional four-year or graduate degree may not be possible or practical. Many community (two-year) college graduates step into higher starting wage brackets than do graduates of liberal arts institutions. The secret is specialized skills.

If your spouse can earn enough to keep you afloat, you might consider enrolling in school full time. In two years you could be employable. If you can't go full time, have a counselor lay out your program and start with one course. The journey of a thousand miles begins with a single step.

Let's talk more about looking for a job. When my friend Hal got his pink slip, he ran for a newspaper. Day after day he scanned the classifieds, making telephone calls, mailing out resumes, going for occasional interviews, doing what most job-seekers do.

Zero. Day after day he drew a blank. All while the bills mounted. The news got around his church that Hal needed a job. A couple of hot tips and he had employment—not what he really wanted, but something to keep him going while he continued to look for better.

Check the classifieds, register at your state unemployment office, and visit employment agencies. But remember, 80 percent of all available jobs never see daylight in these places. Most of the best jobs don't even reach company personnel departments. Even then, you might be beaten out by the friend of an employee.

Hal, for example, was sure after one interview that he had a good job. Good pay and just what he wanted. When the personnel man didn't call back, Hal called him and was told, "Sorry, but when I talked to you, I didn't know that the manager in that division had already hired his wife's uncle."

Repeat ten times for your future benefit: THE BEST JOB LEADS WILL COME FROM PEOPLE I KNOW —MY CONTACTS. Repeat a hundred times if necessary.

As self-employed writers, Marti and I are constantly asked, "How do you get your books published? How do you get communication consulting jobs?" The answer is simply *contacts*. In the nineteen years I've been a full-time writer, I've never placed an ad seeking work.

We believe and so pray that the Lord will lead us to the right people. We then take steps to open the door. We propose an idea for a book to an editor. If we don't know the editor, we find somebody who does and will give us an introduction. Sometimes, when we need work the most, the phone will ring as it did several months ago and a voice will say: "You were recommended by..." (it was a professor who knew our work). At this writing, Marti is in the Philippines researching the book.

Building a reputation takes time. Editors come back to writers with a record of painstaking research, careful writing, and meeting deadlines. Dependability is more important than superior talent when you must choose between the two. Right now I'm working overtime to complete this book and keep a promise to my editor.

If you're out of work, time is not a surplus commodity. You've got to make the right connection soon. So start making your list of people who might be job leads. Your brother-in-law might have an old college roommate who is manager at a place you'd like to work. Get the guy's name. Ask him if he has anything open. If he doesn't, ask if he has any suggestions.

After asking relatives, next check with close friends and neighbors. Look at your Christmas card list. Review old school yearbooks. Jot down the names of old school buddies. That red-headed jokester you used to double-date with might be just the person to put you on a rocket for the future.

I was at a party the other night and stepped back to the fireplace for a bit of warmth. A man standing there introduced himself and asked what I did for a living. That always leads to the next question, "What are you writing about now?" When I told him, he shared this experience.

"My company folded. I happened to have a friend who worked for TVA (Tennessee Valley Authority). He watched the bulletin boards where job openings are posted before being given to employment agencies. When something came up in my field, he got the proper forms for me to fill out. Then he turned them

LIFE CHANGES

in to the manager in that department. That's how I got the good job I have now."

If you're still stuck on square one, and you're a college alumnus, get in touch with the school placement office and alumni association, even if you graduated twenty years ago. They can tell you of job possibilities and where some of your old classmates are now working.

Keep communicating. Call. Write. Don't worry about bothering your contacts. They will feel honored that you asked for job help. Awhile back an editor friend called to say his company was going out of business. Did I know of any editorial jobs elsewhere? He knew I was in touch with a number of religious publishers. It happened that I did know of something. He got the job.

Some of your best referrals may come from church friends. Certainly it's wrong to attend church just for business purposes. But don't let that keep you from asking your Christian friends for help when you need it. Your church may have a bulletin board or a newsletter where you could state your need for a job.

While I can't accept all the doctrine of the Church of Latter Day Saints (Mormons), I admire the way they help members in economic need. A needy Mormon can go to his spiritual leader and get food and money for his family. The local Mormon "stake" (district) has a farm or industry where the unemployed member can work until he gets permanent employment. That's one reason why the Mormons are growing much faster than many other religious groups.

While you're job-looking, read up on how to prepare resumes and succeed in interviews. Here are some pointers from the experts for a professional resume:

1. *Keep it simple, short, and well organized.* No longer than two pages.

2. *Be honest without putting yourself down.* Be prepared if you're asked to document what you've put down.

3. *Tailor the resume to the job.* Identify and underline skills that you think will help you on this job or with this company.

4. *List achievements and awards that are pertinent.* The company probably doesn't care to know that you won a twenty-five dollar savings bond for answering a trivia question from a rock radio station. The company *will* be interested to know that you qualified for the college scholastic society in your field.

5. *Mention volunteer experience if skills relate to the job.*

6. *Leave off these items:* No photos unless specifically required. No personal information unless directly relevant to the job. This includes age, height, weight, marital status, religious affiliations, etc. Omit negative reasons for leaving an earlier job. Don't give references unless you can list a person well known in the field in which you are applying. Just say, "References provided upon request."

7. *Include a personal letter of application.* Simply and briefly request consideration for the position, mention reasons you are interested, and ask for a personal interview.

The resume is a screening mechanism for the employer and a door opener for you. Always follow it up with a phone call or a short note stating that you really would like an interview.

Now for some tips on the interview:

1. *Do your homework.* Research the company, its products, services, and place in the industry. Try to get a copy of the company's annual report before the interview. Look in reference books such as *Dun & Bradstreet* or *Moody's* in the library. Read several issues of the trade magazine in that industry.

2. *Prepare for standard questions.* The interviewer says, "Tell me about yourself," and you

begin, "I was born.... I went to school at...." How much better is: "I've become very interested in.... I've discovered I have some real ability in.... I have some special training in...."

Another stock question is, "Why did you leave your last job?" Negative comments will only weigh in against you. If the company closed because of foreign competition, say so. And you might add, "From that experience I got some ideas that I believe will help this company."

Make a list of questions you expect. Have your spouse or a friend interrogate you. But don't go in with a memorized spiel. Just be ready to express yourself in a positive way that will indicate your knowledge of the company and awareness of abilities in yourself which will advance the firm. Remember, the interviewer is not running an aid office. He's trying to help his company. If he thinks you can make a solid contribution, then you could get the job.

3. *Be assured.* Get a good night's sleep the night before the interview. Eat a hearty breakfast. Read over your resume and information about the company. Arrive ahead of time so you will have time to relax and review your ideas over a cup of coffee. It's like taking a final exam in college. If you're confident you will pass, you probably will.

4. *Dress properly.* A traditional business suit and white shirt are almost always in style for a man seeking a white-collar position. For a blue-collar job, you could not go wrong by wearing a tie. A conservative but fashionable suit or skirt and blouse would be safe for a woman. Generally try to avoid clothing, hairstyles, and jewelry that would be distracting. You want the interviewer to hear and see *you*, not what you're wearing.

5. *Act normal and establish rapport.* If the interviewer wants to talk football for a couple of minutes, go along. But try to stay on safe subjects for small talk.

You're taking chances by volunteering your opinion on politics and controversial social issues. Be personable without trying to become instant buddies. Use last names and proper titles. If the interviewer is a "doctor," address him as such.

6. *Be straightforward, honest, and pleasant.* Look the interviewer in the eye. Answer questions forthrightly. Questions about your age, marital status, and other personal matters are supposed to be illegal. If the interviewer asks them in an oblique way, don't mount a challenge or show resentment. Turn an irritating question into an opportunity, such as: "I am married, of course, but my wife is behind me all the way. She doesn't mind when I have to go out of town on business."

7. *Keep the emphasis on what you can do for the company, not what the company can do for you.* Don't ask about salary, vacations, or pensions in the initial interview. If the interviewer asks you to specify your salary needs, say or write "Negotiable," or "Whatever is fair." Avoid boxing yourself in.

8. *Act enthusiastic but not anxious.* If you've researched the prospective employer, you can show intelligent enthusiasm. It doesn't hurt to brag (honestly) on the company. Just don't give the impression that getting the job is a life-or-death matter for you. You want the interviewer to feel that if the company doesn't get you, it will be the loser.

9. *Send a thank-you letter after you get home.* Briefly reemphasize your interest and enthusiasm for the job. Thank the interviewer for his or her time. Offer to answer any further questions. Give your phone number and say when you can be reached.

10. *Follow up in a week if you haven't heard.* A short note may be better than a phone call, which might give the impression that you're pestering the interviewer. Simply say you're wondering how things are going. Wish the interviewer well. Don't make any demands.

If your first interview doesn't pan out, use the expertise you've gained to do better the next time. Don't take each no as a personal defeat. Keep your chin up. Keep writing letters, sending out resumes, and making phone calls. Advises an employment counselor of Rockford, Illinois: "Keep talking, keep asking. Don't stop. Every 'no' you get is closer to the one 'yes' you're looking for. Just as sure as the Lord made little green apples, there are jobs out there. Yes, even in a depressed area such as Rockford."

Above all, maintain closeness with the Lord. Allow him to walk with you. Scripture says: "Whether therefore ye eat, or drink, or whatsoever ye do, do all to the glory of God" (1 Corinthians 10:31). The job you want, the income you need is for the glory of the Lord. If you really want to please him, he will sustain you until you find the job he has for you.

Back to my friends Harry and Bert. Last week I heard that Harry didn't get the transit bus job. But he did get a bus driver's job with the Tucson school system. This will keep him solvent while he's training for a new career.

Bert was out of work for a year. A temporary job didn't pan out. The other day he called me from his new office. "I got what I wanted," he exulted. "I can even walk to work." Then he added, "Come and see me and I'll buy you the best steak in town."

4

When Adversity Strikes

A terse voice from a black scanner crackles through our house: "Stand by for tones!" Seconds later the signal sounds, followed by the dispatcher's description and the address of the victim. Ours is a small suburban mountain community. Tones may not sound for three days, then ring out three times in an hour. A heart attack, a stroke, an automobile accident, a fall, a child hit by a B.B. gun, an attempted suicide—whatever the problem, two trained volunteers and an ambulance driver from the Waldens Ridge Emergency Service respond. If the tones sound between eleven A.M. and five P.M. on Tuesday or Thursday, Marti dashes for the ambulance.

Not long ago the tones sounded at five A.M. on a Monday morning. A fifty-six-year-old male had suffered a stroke. He was a member of my Sunday school class whom I had sat beside just nineteen hours before. A successful businessman, he had looked to be in glowing health. None of us in the class suspected that a vital artery going to his brain was closing fast. The volunteers sped Hampton to the hospital in the screaming ambulance.

Over a million Americans die from heart and circulatory-related diseases each year. Hampton was not to be one of them. Weeks later he came home, his right arm almost useless, his face thin and drawn, to face the rest of his life with an injured brain.

At this moment two other good friends are in the hospital. A fellow deacon has had major stomach surgery and will be on a strict diet for the rest of his life. A woman friend, who typed the manuscript of several of our books, is being kept alive by dialysis and a respirator. She is only forty-one. If she survives, her life style could be severely limited for the rest of her life.

Neither I nor my wife has been struck by a crippling illness or injury—yet. Serious adversity will one day certainly strike our home and yours. "Man is born unto trouble, as the sparks fly upward" (Job 5:7). The "whole creation groaneth and travaileth in pain" (Romans 8:22). "If you want to live without trouble," said Oliver Wendell Holmes, "you'll have to die young." Adversity will come. Blindness, deafness, stroke, heart attack, cancer, or any of a myriad of other afflictions will hit you or someone dependent on you. Your life will never be the same.

Just a few days ago I learned that strong man Paul Anderson has kidney disease and must be on dialysis. He's also had five major operations in the past two years. How powerful and invincible this man looked (the first human to lift over 6,000 pounds) when I visited in his home a few years ago.

There is no use pretending "it will never happen to me." The big question is: After tragedy strikes and limitations are imposed, what will you do with the rest of your life? Will you withdraw into a shell of self-pity and wait for death that may be years in coming? Will you draw the shades of night and despair around you and shut out all lights of hope?

Six years ago I received a jolting letter from the wife of one of my old seminary pals, one of the funniest guys I ever knew. "Emerson is having to resign his church," Polly Isler wrote. "The doctor has given him less than a year to live."

I remembered Emerson's fading eyesight. He had keritonitis and had to rest his eyes for two hours a day. Even so, he had worked his way through seminary and helped support his widowed mother by working nights as a disc jockey.

During the intervening quarter-century I had seen my old friend only twice: once at a church convention, and once when he came to Chicago, where we were then living, for a cornea transplant. I went to see him there, taking along the galleys of a book of humor which I had dedicated:

> *TO THE REV. EMERSON L. ISLER,*
> *OLD SEMINARY FRIEND,*
> *WHO HAS THE BEST SENSE*
> *AND NONSENSE OF HUMOR*
> *OF ANY PERSON I'VE EVER KNOWN.*

He loved it.

The first transplant, which was to save his left eye from going blind, didn't take. With his right eye deteriorating fast, he began memorizing the New Testament from records. He intended to continue in the ministry.

His doctor found another donor, a six-year-old boy, for his failed left eye. "My antibodies put up a terrible fight." He laughed over the phone. "But they lost the battle. My sight is almost perfect in this eye. Glorious!" Then he got a new cornea in his right eye. Now he had almost perfect vision in both eyes.

Emerson spoke frequently to Lions' clubs, encouraging them in their campaigns for better eye care and treatment. He always expressed his faith: "God had a purpose in the disease that was making me go blind. His timetable was never too slow or too fast. As each eye got worse, he provided just the help I needed."

We stayed in touch by mail and phone, although I was not to see Emerson again for several years. In 1974 he became pastor of Glenn Street Baptist Church in Newberry, South Carolina. For the first time in his career, he did not have to moonlight as a radio anouncer, nor did Polly have to work outside the home. Their oldest daughter, Linda, was ready for college and their youngest, Ann, was doing well in the fifth grade. Emerson wrote that the church was growing and that he had a thirty-minute radio program every weekday called "Joyful Moments." How gratifying it was to hear that my old friend, at forty-seven, was at last to the point where he could utilize all his talents in the Lord's work. Surely, after all his suffering, he deserved some good times.

Then, just a few weeks later, he collapsed while jogging. Tests indicated he had come close to a heart attack. "You must slow down," the doctor insisted.

Foolishly, after only a few days' rest, Emerson jumped right back into harness. The next time he had to have bypass surgery. Three months later he was back in his pulpit, stubbornly believing that he could continue preaching. A third collapse put him back in the hospital with an ultimatum to accept the seriousness of his illness or die.

He handed his written resignation to a deacon visiting from the church. Then he turned his face to the wall and surrendered to anger and depression. "I was mad with God, myself, my family, everybody," he told me later. "My life was over."

One morning his elderly nurse stopped in. "Do I understand that you're a preacher?"

"Yes," Emerson snapped grumpily.

"Well, you certainly haven't been acting like a man of God!" With that, she turned and slammed the door behind her.

A few minutes later Emerson heard the door slowly open again. "Forgive me if I upset you, Pastor. I believe you're a man of God. I just wanted to make you realize that you aren't having the faith you should have in this crisis."

"That was the turning point," Emerson said afterwards. "I turned my life over to the Lord. No matter what happened, I vowed to accept whatever else he had for me."

To his surprise the church refused to accept his resignation. They pledged to get "supply" preachers to fill the pulpit until Emerson could return. By carefully conserving his strength, he was actually able to preach a few more Sundays. Then he went back for a catherization procedure and learned that the bypass surgery had failed. The cardiologist grimly informed him: "You're worse than you were before."

"How long do I have?"

"I doubt if you'll go a year," the doctor said.

That was when Polly wrote me and other friends that Emerson was terminal.

Emerson insisted on preaching one last Sunday. His subject: "God Has the Last Word!" Then he walked slowly down to the fellowship hall where church members and other friends from the community were gathering to honor him with a going-away party. The deacon chairman handed him a thousand-dollar check and promised that the church would continue to provide $100 a week until further notice.

Taking permanent disability, he and Polly moved to a little house on a pine-studded half acre in Columbia, South Carolina. Marti and I visited them there one cool fall day.

Our old friends greeted us exuberantly. I asked Emerson about his health. "Oh, my eyesight is the best ever," he grinned. "Of course, I have this little heart problem. I can walk around the house. Sometimes I can make it to the mailbox. But I'm not complaining. It was six years ago that the doctor gave me just one year. I'm living on bonus time."

Their youngest daughter was now in college, their oldest married. Polly had gone back to work to supplement Emerson's pension. He is alone from 7:45 A.M. to 5:40 P.M. "I never know if I'm going to find him alive when I get home," she worried. "We just go from day to day."

Polly told us about her work in a state hospital for patients over fifty-five. "Every day I counsel with stroke victims, amputees, people suffering from dementia and other problems. I tell them, 'Accept what you can do and can't do. Be realistic.'"

She cited a former airline consultant who used to travel all over the world. "He's had a stroke and broken his hip. His speech is impaired and he's in a wheelchair. When I come in, he wheels down to meet me. He holds my tote bag while I unlock my office door. It helps him to help me. That's something he can do."

What is Emerson doing with the rest of his life, besides staying home all day? He has a radio "studio" in a section of their den. "When I left Newberry, the church was paying for my thirty-minute program," he said. "The manager said I could continue the program free until I died. He didn't know I would live this long! A few months later he gave me the station's daily five-minute devotional. Since then five other stations have joined our 'Joyful Moments' network."

Emerson's studio includes microphones, turntables, mixer, and tape duplicators. The equipment is a gift from a former church member. Christian record companies provide records. "Polly and I buy the tapes and pay the postage for mailing to the stations," he said. "We ask only prayer from our listeners."

He cued up a tape and I heard the familiar voice, vibrant and resonant as ever: "You're on the joyline with ... Joyful Moments." The program that followed featured sacred music interspersed by inspirational vignettes, Scripture, and devotional thoughts. Polly is also a writer and hopes to publish some of Emerson's radio material in a book.

The shelves in the studio are lined with tapes and books. Recent listener letters are stacked on a desk.

"Quite a few write after hearing me say that I'm disabled with a heart condition. Some have a crippling disease or injury and think their life is over. I try to help them believe that God has a plan for every life. Each of us, I say, no matter how crippled we may be, has some talent, some ability in that plan. Looking back, I can see how the Lord guided me every step of the way. I was first involved in radio. Then I became a pastor and continued broadcasting as a hobby and income supplement. Now the Lord has put me back in radio full time."

Emerson popped a nitroglycerin pill under his tongue—the sixth for the day, he admitted—which is supplemented by about fifteen other daily medications. He's also a diabetic. "Sure, at times I long for good health. Some nights I dream that I'm back in the pulpit, preaching to big crowds. But really, I'm happy the way I am. And I cherish every birthday.

"I tell people who have a crippling health problem: 'Don't try to hide your condition. On the other hand, don't dwell on it and complain about your limitations. Accept yourself the way you are and go on.'"

We took a cassette program for the road. From the car speakers boomed his voice, "You're on the joyline...." Then his theme song, "Let's Just Praise the Lord...." Living on borrowed time, Emerson is speaking to more people than he ever reached in a pulpit ministry —and without having to leave his house.

When the program ended, we mulled over a seeming contradiction in Emerson: Why, after suffering from failing eyesight all his life, had it been so difficult for him to accept his heart disease? Perhaps it was his vocation. A blind man could continue to preach. A man with a failing heart could never enter the pulpit ministry again.

Also, he had always talked openly about his

eyes, even joked about them. He had spoken to the Lions' clubs. He had tried to help others with eye problems. But when the heart surgery failed, he rebelled and became bitter, refusing even to discuss the implications with his wife. Only after accepting his heart disability as within the plan of God could he start rebuilding for the rest of his life. Only when he admitted his condition to family and friends could he learn to live with a diseased heart.

Others who have gone through the deep waters of life-limiting adversity have told me the order of their responses were much like Emerson's—denial, rebellion, bitterness, and depression.

Eight years ago I sat in the office of Forrest Cate, a Chattanooga Ford dealer, and listened to his story of victory over adversity:

"I was student body president in college. I married 'Miss Chattanooga.' We had three beautiful children. I was vice president of the Jaycees and just beginning to get on my feet in business when a blur suddenly appeared in my left eye. A doctor told me a tiny blood vessel had ruptured and I had diabetic retinopathy. It was too late for laser surgery. Within a few months I was blind in both eyes.

"I worried myself sick over whether I could be blind and run my business. How could I pay my debts and care for my family? I almost went crazy, asking, 'Why me, God?' It seemed so unfair. Here I was trying to be a good Christian husband, father, businessman, and employer, while people I knew who broke every rule in the book seemed to have no problems.

"I had some well-meaning friends," Forrest recalled, "who just knew I must have committed some terrible sin. They had me confess every sin I could think of and then some.

"I guess I would have gone mad if my dear wife, Marcia, had not kept assuring me of God's love and comfort. She kept telling me that God must have some purpose in my life.

"Then one afternoon I came home and found a cassette tape of a sermon on suffering by Ben Haden. Someone had come by and dropped it off—I never knew who it was. I put the tape in a player and listened. Ben's text was from John 9 where Jesus' disciples asked of the man born blind, 'Who did sin, this man or his parents?' Jesus answered that the man was blind 'that the works of God should be made manifest in him.' The preacher was talking right to me when he said a suffering believer should try to find some works for God to manifest in his life.

"I knelt down and asked God to show me what a blind man could do for him, and how I could help someone else. A few days later one of my salesmen asked if I would speak at his church's Wednesday evening prayer service. I described my struggles and read what Jesus said to the man born blind. A woman stopped me on the way out and said, 'My dear mother is dying of cancer. Tonight you showed me why God has not healed her.'

"Somebody in that church told someone in another church about me. Soon I was speaking almost every week." He reached down to pat his faithful seeing-eye dog and chuckled. "Romulus, here, has got to be the church-goingest dog in town."

Forrest had a large dealership with over a hundred employees.

"How do you handle your business?" I asked.

"I really think my blindness has helped. I feel a deeper love for my fellowman. I have more rapport with my employees. Every morning, when I come in, Romulus and I walk through the departments, greeting each one. I just assume they're all smiling at me. I come into the office and my secretary goes over the mail, sales figures, and other business with me. I receive visitors just as I always have. My secretary is instructed never to tell anyone I'm blind. One out-of-town salesman came in here three times before realizing I couldn't see."

I saw Forrest the first time in 1974. During the next three years his annual sales jumped from five to fifteen million dollars. Year after year he won Ford's Distinguished Achievement Award. He resumed his hobby of competing in Tennessee's famed walking horse shows. He wore tiny earphones tuned to a transistor held by a trainer who sat on a fence and gave instructions. "Pull on the right rein," the trainer would say. "Tighten up a bit. Pull to the right. Canter." In the annual big event, Forrest won second place in a field of sighted riders.

I often saw Forrest and Romulus on TV doing commercials. They did network spots for the American Diabetic Foundation. Forrest came to our church and gave his testimony in a sermon called, "Walking by Faith and Not by Sight."

The years passed. The Cates transferred their membership to our church. One evening I met Forrest coming in to the Wednesday church supper and asked how he was doing. "Praising the Lord." He smiled. "I just came back from speaking to the Diabetic Foundation in St. Louis. Some people were planning to introduce a resolution banning prayer and the mention of God's name in the annual meeting. They brought their supporters to the closing session when they thought the crowd would be small and it would be easy to get the bylaw passed. That happened to be when I gave my testimony. The Lord touched so many hearts that they didn't dare make a move."

I got my food and brought my plate to where he was sitting. Marcia put his plate before him and arranged the portions by imaginary points on the clock. "I've got this down perfect," he chuckled, balancing a scoop of peas on his fork. "Well, not quite," he admitted.

"Blindness has its limitations which I've learned to accept. I've always been very independent. Never wanted anybody to help me. Now somebody has to arrange my food, pick out my clohes, and drive me to work.

"If I could just see one sunset," he said wistfully. "Tell Marcia one more time how lovely she looks in a new dress. See my little girl dolled up at a school affair. Being blind isn't the most pleasant thing. But it's brought some pluses, and for that I'm thankful."

One afternoon I was driving up Mountain Creek Road, near the Cates' home. Just ahead I saw a man and a big tan dog jogging. Forrest and Romulus. "Getting my evening exercise," Forrest said later.

One night Forrest and Marcia came to our home for a prayer meeting. He sat near the hi-fi, his face turned toward the group, giving no appearance of blindness. "Lord, I've got so many things to thank you for, I don't know where to begin," he prayed. There were a lot of wet "seeing" eyes that night.

Not long afterward, Forrest went into the hospital. No visitors except the family were allowed. The surgeon found a large tumor in his brain. My friend lingered on for a few weeks, then one day, I fancy the Lord said, "Forrest, you've been blind long enough. Come up here where you can see."

We joined the immense crowd at the funeral home. The line to view the body stretched far into the parking lot. It was as though the governor had died. I thought again of what Jesus said about the man born blind: "Neither hath this man sinned, nor his parents: but that the works of God should be made manifest in him" (John 9:3). Thousands had seen the "works of God" in blind Forrest Cate.

Forrest often said, "Marcia has a harder time than I do." Perhaps so. When a spouse, child, or dependent parent is disabled, the loved one will experience emotional shock. Some will suffer guilt. The caring person's options in living are lessened, the life style altered.

My daddy was always an outdoorsman. I treasure childhold memories of accompanying him on coon hunts, fishing excursions, and camping trips. He bought, trained, and sold coon hounds for several years, then worked as a fishing guide on Lake Bull Shoals in the Ozarks. Most of Mother's time, after they moved from the farm, was spent tending their little rural store.

Mother's illness, coming after both of them had retired, was a severe blow to him. She was diagnosed as having Alzheimer's Disease, Parkinson's, and diabetes. All incurable. Daddy suffered an emotional breakdown, partly because he was unable to take care of her. Knowing she was unable to care for herself, we children had to place her in the little county seat nursing home. After Daddy recovered from his illness, he was able to visit her every day.

After three months she improved enough so that Daddy could again care for her at home. Of course, with Alzheimer's disease her memory and presence of mind will increasingly worsen. She will eventually have to go back to the nursing home.

Daddy is his old self again. He can drive Mother to visit the children who live nearby. But he or someone in the family must always be with her. I talked to him on the phone a few nights ago. He said he hadn't been hunting or fishing in months. He had sold his last dog. "My job is to take care of your mama now," he said.

He doesn't complain. They've been together over fifty years, raised eight children, seen hard times and good times. For a man who loves the woods and streams, his road is hard. But love paves the way. So long as he can care for Mother, Daddy will spend the rest of his life with her.

I know couples who have agonized over whether to institutionalize or keep at home a severely handicapped child. In either case, their lives are never the same again. If the child remains at home, the mother usually bears the greatest burden. So long as the child lives or is at home, she cannot live as other mothers. Nor can the family be as free as other families. If they choose an institution, the heartache will always be with them, and for some the guilt will linger over wondering if they should have separated themselves from the child.

T.B. and Essie Mae Maston were married over half a century ago. Essie Mae almost lost her life giving birth to their cerebral palsied son, Thomas McDonald. Back then, institutional care was less available than now. Essie Mae probably wouldn't have put Tom Mac in a hospital anyway.

She cared for their boy while T.B. completed his doctoral work at Yale University and became a seminary professor. Later she cared for her widowed mother for seventeen years. "When the load was heaviest, she never complained," T.B. recalled.

Through the years, Essie Mae somehow managed to teach a Sunday school class and visit members while T.B. stayed home with Tom Mac and caught up on classwork. She also spent a lot of time in her garden, keeping a close eye on the boy. "I can bury a lot of self-pity in my flower beds," she once told a group of young wives.

T.B. is retired now. Tom Mac, fifty-five years old, is still with them. The three can travel together. They've been to the Middle East and South America were T.B. has spoken to missionaries and national pastors.

T.B. Maston is a revered name to hundreds of Southern Baptist pastors whom he taught at Southwestern Baptist Theological Seminary in Fort Worth. Some took their doctorates under him in ethics, T.B.'s field, and are now leaders in their denomination. One of his "doctors," the pastor of a large metropolitan church, told me, "T.B. Maston is the greatest Christian I ever knew."

T.B. never takes credit. He says of his wife, "Just as God made our lives one many years ago, so our accomplishments in life are one." Essie Mae, he thinks, "could have succeeded in almost any vocation or profession of her choosing," but chose to devote herself to her crippled son and her husband.

The Bible has much to say about the value of suffering. Trials produce endurance, perseverance, character, hope (Romans 5:3, 4; James 1:3). Faith that is tested by fire may "result in praise and glory and honor at the revelation of Jesus Christ" (1 Peter 1:7, NASB). The "God of all comfort... comforts us in all our affliction so that we may be able to comfort those who are in any affliction with the comfort with which we ourselves are comforted by God" (2 Corinthians 1:3, 4, NASB).

Scripture says that suffering, as painful as it may be, is good for us in the long run. That does not take away the agony. Nor does it provide all the answers to the "whys" which keep coming.

Lives there the man or woman who has never asked, "Why am I suffering?" There is not one sufferer who has not screamed from the depths, "Why me? What purpose is in this for the rest of my life?"

"The worst suffering," Dr. James Mallory, the noted Atlanta Christian psychiatrist, told me, "is not in the pain but our inability to find meaning in it. Nietzsche wrote, 'He who has a why to live for can bear almost any how.' That is certainly true."

Dr. Mallory cited five often interrelated major causes of suffering:

> Natural effects of living in a fallen, sinful world.
> Satanic oppression.

Having done something contrary to God's will.

Somebody else has done something contrary to the will of God.

God is seeking to change or guide you through a process that involves suffering.

How you react is crucial, he said. Normally, your defenses go up; you may try to deny the problem, blame others, play martyr, and wallow in self-pity. If these "tricks" aren't convincing, your defenses may go down. You may then become more and more significantly open to change.

"You begin to reevaluate your life style, priorities, decisions, and attitudes," Dr. Mallory continued. "You see things about yourself you never saw before, some of which you don't like. It is in this setting that you can become open to change, positive or negative, constructive or destructive.

"You are at a crossroads. One road leads to discouragement, despair, depression, cynicism, and all sorts of destructive attitudes. The other road leads to hope, faith, growth, and confidence" (*Untwisted Living,* Victor Books, 1982, p. 53).

At this time you can rebel or adopt what Dr. Mallory calls "the thanksgiving principle" by affirming that you believe God really loves you, that you belong to him, and that he will take you through the suffering situation. You "know that God causes all things to work together for good to those who love God, to those who are called according to His purpose" (Romans 8:28, NASB).

Jacqueline Mayer Townsend was voted "Miss America" in 1962. After her year of glory, she married, had two beautiful children, and settled down to enjoy the life of a happy housewife. In 1970, when she was only twenty-eight, she awoke unable to speak, her right side paralyzed. After barely surviving a major stroke, she had to learn again how to read, speak, dress herself, and even dial the telephone.

Over a decade later, she's still rebuilding her life.

The stroke has made her "grow much as a person." In sharing her experience, she says, "God guides me and helps me. He has a plan for me—to give other people hope."

Giving others hope. Helping other sufferers find reasons to go on living. What more meaningful way for one bowed down by adversity to spend the rest of his life?

Giving others hope summons the picture of my friend Howard Shoemake, a strapping six-foot-four missionary about whom I wrote a book several years ago. Down in the Dominican Republic, the tall Texan is a national hero for medical programs and other mercy efforts which saved thousands of lives. Just the mere mention of his name may have saved me from serious injury, even death, at the hands of a mob of students one afternoon. They had accused me of being a CIA agent. When I said I was writing a book about missionary Shoemake, they dropped the spy charge.

For five years now the celebrated missionary has suffered from cancer of the bone marrow and the skin. His vertebrae have been fractured in six places. He has suffered from chronic kidney failure, a duodenal ulcer, heart insufficiency, and hypertension. During the past year, he has been hospitalized three times and has had forty-six skin cancers plucked from his face, arms, and neck.

Howard is able to wear a body brace and somehow walk. Between hospitalizations, he encourages fellow cancer patients at Baylor University Medical Center. Neatly dressed in a business suit, he slips into a room and tells a discouraged patient: "Look here. What you have isn't a death sentence. I've had cancer for five years and am making it. If you'll just trust your doctor and the Lord, maybe things will change for the better."

Dr. Lloyd Kitchens, Howard's oncologist, says the positive attitude of a cancer victim can make a difference with fellow sufferers. "It's quite a shock to learn you have cancer and must undergo treatment that's frequently pretty tough. It helps to see someone who has had it, has done all right, and is still going about his business."

Howard's wife, Dorothy Dell, makes "rounds" with him. She is an encouragement to spouses who must sit by and watch their mates suffer. Before Howard's illness, he was so busy in his work that they seldom saw one another before bedtime. "Now we're together almost all the time," she says.

"That's good," Howard agrees. "In many ways, my illness has brought the best years of our lives."

Cancer, stroke, heart attack, blindness, deafness, serious injury, or some other crippling adversity need not be the end, but the beginning of a marvelous new chapter in your life. For both the sufferer and his loved one, the great trouble can lead to deeper relationships with a touch of heaven.

Furthermore, the very experience, which seems at the moment to have snuffed out your most cherished hopes, could turn you in a new direction of blessing you never dreamed possible.

Dr. A. J. Cronin had a thriving and well-paying medical practice in London when he began having severe attacks of indigestion. He consulted a colleague and was told he had a chronic duodenal ulcer. An immediate and complete rest of six months was mandatory, or he might die.

Dr. Cronin had long had a strange "urge to be a writer." He took his family to a cottage "amidst green meadows sheltered by a wild grandeur of mountains." There he wrote his first novel, *The Citadel*. It was translated into twenty-one languages, selling over three million copies, and was serialized, dramatized, and filmed. Cronin's illness marked the beginning of one of the greatest literary careers in the twentieth century.

More recently a beautiful girl in the bloom of youth broke her neck in a diving accident. Joni Eareckson could move only her head. She wanted to close her eyes and die. But a flame of hope, ignited by a spiritual commitment, would not go out. She learned to paint holding the brush between her teeth. Her work caught the attention of a television producer. My editor friend Al Bryant saw her on the "Today" show. The rest is history. Her book, telling of what she is doing with her life since the accident, has sold over three million copies and been made into a major motion picture.

The other afternoon I was driving home from the library and heard her program, "Joni and Friends," on the car radio. She was talking about the spiritual body of believers, how Christ is the head and we are the members. "Sometimes we in the body block ourselves off from getting directions from our Head," she said. "I can understand that. My head has all kinds of great ideas for my body. Unfortunately, my body can't respond because my spine is permanently injured. Fortunately, that need not happen to me in the spiritual realm. By yielding and obeying, I can keep the channels open to the leadership of my Lord."

Barry Lipin was just twenty-six when a rare nerve disease sent him into the world of silence. Unable to pursue the law career he had planned, he drifted aimlessly for eight years, remembering beautiful music and the voices of loved ones, and bemoaning his deafness.

Then he determined to "put my chin up and fight." He learned to read lips and went into the auto leasing business. The business prospered into a multi-million-dollar enterprise. As Forrest Cate did in his auto dealership, Barry Lupin hasn't let his handicap keep him from normal work. When a customer calls, his secretary picks up an extension phone. She hears the caller and mouths the words silently to Barry, who sits nearby. He replies in normal speech. Callers are never told that Barry is stone deaf.

"If you have a physical handicap, you can run into a corner and hide," says Barry. "Or you can just try harder than the next man and make a success of yourself."

Herman Gockel lost his voice at thirty-two. A shattering experience for a young preacher. He consulted twenty-five different specialists. None could help.

Herman resigned his church on an Easter Sunday. He took his wife Mildred and two children to live with his widowed mother in Cleveland, Ohio. Mildred got a secretarial job. Herman stayed home with the children.

As he did housework, a Bible verse kept coming to mind: "He who did not spare his own Son but gave him up for us all, will he not also give us all things?" (Romans 8:32, RSV). Above the darkness and gloom, Herman saw a star of hope.

He prayed. He believed. Six months later he got a job answering mail for Dr. Walter Maier's "Lutheran Hour" radio broadcast. He also wrote rhymes for Christmas cards and helped in the shipping department at Concordia Publishing House.

Two years later Herman was manager of Corcordia. He wrote ads, prepared catalogs, developed book jackets, designed Sunday church bulletins, and helped launch several new Christian magazines.

Then Mildred became critically ill. Twenty-six times she was hospitalized. Six times she came to the brink of death. Herman kept believing Romans 8:32. His books and articles inspired millions.

Herman was asked to develop a new TV

program for his church. "This Is the Life" became a milestone in religious communications.

All after a preacher lost his voice.

Tired, depressed, discouraged? Take heart. God is not done with you yet. We used to sing a song in youth revivals:

> *Got any rivers you think are uncrossable?*
> *Got any mountains you can't tunnel through?*
> *God specializes in things thought impossible;*
> *And he can do what no other power can do.*

Then comes the challenge: "Let go and let God have His wonderful way...."

The greatest men and women seem to have suffered the most. Remember the Apostle Paul's celebrated "thorn in the flesh"? We are not told the ailment. It could have been failing eyesight, epilepsy, piercing headaches, hearing impairment, or something else. He "besought the Lord" three times that it might depart. How did God answer? "He said unto me," wrote Paul, " 'My grace is sufficient for you: for my strength is made perfect in weakness.' "

How did the great apostle respond? "Most gladly therefore will I rather glory in my infirmities, that the power of Christ may rest upon me" (2 Corinthians 12:7-9). He "let go and let God" have his wonderful way.

Your life is only over if you think it is. You can learn to "glory" in your infirmities and build a bridge out of them to find God's purpose for the rest of your life.

Think about....

Bill Wilson, a "hopeless alcoholic," founding Alcoholics Anonymous, which has brought sobriety to millions.

John Milton doing his greatest literary work after he became blind at forty-four.

Corrie ten Boom becoming a world inspiration, with her books and films. She had been released from a Nazi concentration camp in her fifties, after she had lost her entire family.

Ludwig von Beethoven creating his greatest symphonies after he started going deaf. Vowed the music master: "I will seize life by the throat."

But you need not draw inspiration from just the famous. Draw from the example of LaRue Moss who was told by her father when she left for college, "Honey, if you're going to reach out for the stars, first you have to put out your hand."

LaRue aspired to be an educator. First she fell in love. Six weeks after the wedding she broke her back in a car wreck. It was three years before she could walk again.

She almost died in childbirth and was bedridden for a year.

Finally she went back and completed her bachelor's degree in elementary education—sixteen years after her father had first taken her to the bus station to leave for college. She attended school while operating a lawn mowing business to help support her family.

She enrolled for a master's while continuing to mow lawns. She was studying for her doctorate at Vanderbilt University in Nashville when a hit-and-run driver struck her down. Despite chest injuries and a bruised heart, she managed to stay in graduate school.

A dull backache continued and intensified. The doctor said she might be paralyzed within twenty-four hours if she didn't have surgery. Leaving her incomplete dissertation, she was whisked into the operating room.

She awoke in a sunlit yellow room to see the beaming faces of her family. "I thought I had died and gone to heaven," she said. Then, looking at her sister, she asked, "Hey, did you bring my dissertation back from the waiting room?"

Sixteen months later this brave woman who kept "reaching for the stars" received her doctorate in education.

Take God. Take hold. Move out. Reach up. Reach for the stars. Let God make something beautiful out of your life.

5

When You Lose a Spouse

Rex was thirty-six years old when a small malignancy was discovered in his wife Marie's lower intestine. Rex, a veteran broadcaster before becoming a missionary, had just finished building a missionary radio station in an Asian country. He brought Marie back to the U.S. for surgery. Her prognosis after the operation was quite good. "If she remains free from symptoms for five years," the doctor said, "she's home free."

"Five years to the month," Rex told me one morning at breakfast, "X-rays showed shadows on both lungs. They gave her five or six months to live, which turned out to be the time she lived."

Marie's death left Rex with three young daughters—eleven, thirteen, and fifteen, and memories of a "nearly perfect, textbook marriage."

"My husband was found to have a heart condition just before his retirement from International Nickel," Peggy Poor said when I saw her in Tucson. "The doctors said it wasn't life threatening and that we could look forward to a good retirement. Three short years later he died suddenly and unexpectedly. Two months later my daddy died, making my future look pretty bleak."

When Harriet Thompson called her husband to the breakfast table one morning, she had no inkling that the next few minutes would alter her life. Harriet and

Bill had been married twenty years, exactly half of Harriet's lifetime. They had seen their ups and downs, but overall Harriet felt they had a good marriage. They had three growing children. Bill was doing well in his business. There wasn't a cloud on the horizon for Harriet until Bill put down his fork and announced, "I have to tell you that I no longer love you." "Just like that," Harriet recalled softly, "he walked out of my life forever."

Harvey, thirty-two, was happily married (he thought), the proud father of two preschoolers, and doing well in his company. One day out of the clear blue, his wife Jennie packed her bag, left him and the children, and drove away to "do my own thing." Harvey has not seen her since.

Death and divorce are all around us. Over a million couples will get divorced this year. Almost two million Americans will die. Many will leave widowed spouses, most of whom will be women. I recall a prayer group that met in our home four years ago: six couples, two in their forties, three in the fifty age range, and one pair over sixty. Three of the six men have since died, leaving three grieving widows. Only Marti and I and two other couples remain together.
For some of the widowed, parting may come as the culmination of a long illness; for others, as the result of sudden death. For some of the divorced, the marriage may be dissolved after a lengthy estrangement; for others, the legal breakup of the marriage may be dizzyingly swift. Whether the sundering is long expected or strikes like a thunderbolt in the night, the widowed and the divorced must begin a new chapter in life—alone.
Such stark, cold statistics may mean little until your spouse is gone. Then it becomes personal, and perhaps emotionally shattering.
Psychiatrist Thomas H. Holmes constructed an

emotional stress and disease scale to measure stressful happenings in the journey of life. From his research, he ranked as most stressful the death of a spouse, then divorce. Next came being fired, retirement, change in financial state, and thirty-seven other events bringing marked stress. His findings have been replicated many times by other social scientists. Two notable statistics for the first year after divorce and widowhood stand out: The average divorcee, during the first year after a divorce, experiences twelve times more illnesses and accidents than the average for the general population. Widowers in the forty-fifty age range are 50 percent more likely to die than their married counterparts.

Divorce is a statement of failure. Who can forget Ann Landers' poignant admission: "The sad, incredible fact is that after thirty-six years of marriage Jules and I are being divorced.... How did it happen that something so good for so long didn't last forever? The lady with all the answers does not know the answer to this one."

Still, divorce is the result of a decision by one, or is agreed upon by both parties. Some parties will remarry.

The death of a spouse holds no hope of reunion, short of heaven. The spouse that remains is left with only memories and some heart-rending regrets of what might have been.

Psychiatrists speak of the four stages through which a widowed person typically passes: disbelief, depression, acceptance, and rebuilding. The same is probably true for many divorced persons, although for some, divorce may come as a relief or release from a horrible marriage.

While the believer may come through faster and emerge with more hope and purpose for the future, he or she is not exempt from the agony of loss. For some believers, who mistakenly thought their faith gave them immunity from suffering, the heartache may be greater.

As we sat at breakfast that cold morning in Wheaton, Illinois, my friend Rex talked about the death of his beloved Marie, some twenty years past, as if it were yesterday. "There's nothing about being a Christian that prevents you from any loss, suffering, or agony that anybody else has," he added. "Nothing! Absolutely nothing. No Christian can assume a guaranteed ticket to perennial health and happiness. We ought to know that from reading about Job and Paul in the Bible.

"When I learned Marie had cancer, I assumed God would heal her. I still had that confidence when she was given five or six months to live. We were well-known missionaries. I was a popular Bible teacher and a Christian author. Hundreds were praying for Marie. Some of our friends laid hands on her, assuring her they had messages directly from God that she would recover. I was so sure that I made extensive notes on her illness, intending to write a book called *Diary of a Miracle*. It made no sense that God would let her die.

"When she did, I couldn't accept it. I distinctly remember screaming, 'God, you wouldn't do this to me. I just know you wouldn't. Am I not the guy who sold his business and home and took his family to Asia for you? God, this can't be happening!' I literally rolled on the floor in my agony."

Margaret Rinsma of Stockbridge, Massachusetts, was a counselor to the dying at a hospice when she lost her husband Cornelius to a heart attack after forty-three years of marriage. She thought she was ready for his death, but his death left her almost paralyzed. "I couldn't dial the telephone," she admitted. Three years later she was still not over the loss. "It's like having a part of your body torn out without an anesthetic."

"I still find it very hard to talk about my husband's death," a widow in Missouri lamented to me.

Her pastor husband had died from a heart attack four years before. "It was such a shock that I don't even remember when the children arrived to console me."

Cathy Kammas recalled to counselor Fran White (*Christianity Today*, February 5, 1982) that her husband was just getting adjusted to retirement when he suffered a fatal heart attack. "It took me two years," she said, "before I could 'let go' of him, accept our shared memories as a source of strength rather than a devastation, and take a new interest in life."

Frances Jerz, sixty-five, told *Chicago Sun-Times* columnist Roger Simon that after three years "a day has never passed when I haven't cried.... I say to God, "What did you do to him? Didn't he deserve a little gravy in his life?" Mr. Jerz had been a machine operator and was approaching retirement when he succumbed to cancer.

Every Sunday Mrs. Jerz gets dressed up "like he's there to see me. My daughter drives me to the cemetery. I touch the stone and I feel like he's close to me. That crypt's got the most lipstick on it. I kiss it every time I'm there."

The reality of divorce can also be terribly difficult. It can be especially hard for the wronged person, the one who could not believe it would happen.

I know a woman of sixty, mother of six, grandmother of twelve. Her husband left her over thirty years ago after their sixth child was born. I was in her home not long ago and she talked as if he had never left. She still cannot admit that he has remarried.

A matronly woman breakfasts alone in a southern city. Her daughters will call in a few minutes to chat. One of the grandchildren may stop by. It's easier when one of her loved ones is there, but the pain remains.

Her ex-husband was a well-known evangelist for over twenty years. Thousands were converted under his preaching. His books and records sold in the hundreds of thousands. She shared the limelight. The daughters and their husbands were involved in his ministry. People talked about what an inspiration they were, a family serving the Lord together.

She refused to believe the rumors at first. Her husband was traveling with another woman. Somebody had seen him drinking alcohol on a plane, the other woman by his side. When he came home, he denied all this. She believed him until friends whom she absolutely trusted told her it was all true.

A reporter called to ask about her prominent husband's problems. He asked if she objected to a story. "No," she said, "I just pray it will bring him to his senses."

The article didn't. It did shatter his reputation in Christian circles. Instead of returning to her, he pressed for a divorce, to which she consented.

The preacher is remarried now. His first wife sees him occasionally on television. He continues to be a popular personality. His first wife has only memories, a financial settlement, and the children who still pray for their daddy.

Oh, the ache of losing a loved one through a divorce you did not want!

It's hard to give a loved one up. If you're widowed, your first instinct may be to keep everything just as he left it. His razor and lotion in the bathroom. His suits in the closet. His ties on the rack. His shoes on the shelf. "Oh, the shoes!" exclaimed Elisabeth Elliot after the death of her second husband. "Molded in the always recognizable shape of his feet."

You can't bear to clean out his closet and empty his drawers—a normal reaction in grieving widowhood.

But eventually you *must* get on with the rest of your life, and the sooner the better. Keep some mementos, of course. To try and blot out all memories of him is no solution. But don't deny reality or fear that you're being unfaithful to your loved one. Give away the clothes. If you're a woman, put your initials on the mailbox and in the telephone directory (don't advertise that you're a woman alone). He will always remain in your heart. If you're both believers there will be a reunion in heaven. You must *now* begin building for the rest of *this* life.

Nobody says that adjustments and rebuilding after the death or divorce of a spouse will be easy. You'll have to deal with legal settlements for a divorce, wills and insurance policies (in cases of widowhood). If you can't handle the financial matters yourself, get someone you can trust. If you don't have a lawyer, ask your pastor to recommend one.

You may need counseling. Start with your pastor or a friend's minister. One evening backstage at the Grand Ole Opry, performer Vic Willis shared some of his heartbreak with me. First he lost his father, then two brothers. A year later, two more brothers were found to have cancer; then his remaining brother became critically ill with emphysema. While dealing with these losses and burdens, his marriage broke up. "I had a nervous breakdown and went into deep depression," Vic recalled. "I blamed myself for everything. I prayed for forgiveness, but couldn't forgive myself."

After a stay in a psychiatric unit, Vic refused to return to the hospital. He was contemplating suicide when his ex-wife suggested an entertainer friend's pastor. The pastor listened to his story and said, "Vic, you're killing yourself with this guilt. Everybody else has forgiven you. You've asked God to forgive you. But you won't forgive yourself."

Vic realized his problem. After more talks with the pastor and conversations with lay counselors in the church, Vic reached the point where he could say, "I *feel* forgiven."

Failure to express grief often prevents a survivor from coming to grips with the way things are. You need to express your heartache, declare your loneliness, vent your bitterness to God. Tell him everything.

Psychiatrist James Mallory points to the biblical prophets Habakkuk (3:16-19) and Jeremiah (Lamentations 3) as models for breaking these bonds. "Jeremiah pours out his anger and hurt at God in one hard-hitting metaphor after another.... Likewise, the Prophet Habakkuk expressed his disappointment and dismay over seemingly insurmountable burdens and problems:

> These men are utterly honest. They spew it out. Not to manipulate. Not simply to be the biggest martyr that ever lived. But to be healed.
>
> Bringing it out in the light enabled them to accept the healing and cleansing of God ... they're not playing games, putting on a spiritual victory mask, or isolating themselves from God and the body of believers. They bring their hurt out into the light because they know God is there and will do something. Even in their arguments, they don't doubt His existence, they don't like the way He is handling things. And they say so. But they are still putting themselves ultimately under His Lordship (*Untwisted Living*, Victor Books, pp. 5, 6).

Share your grief with others. Real friends will allow you to open up and voice your sorrow. Cathy Kammas found her "real healing when a younger couple recognized my despair and encouraged me to talk about my loneliness and express my outrage that this should happen to me. I started to recognize that part of my grieving was even over my own inevitable death and shortness of life. It freed me to live again. Maybe that's what helped pull me out of the depression. At that point I found myself taking more initiative."

Having to care for children pulls some mourners through. Harvey conceded that the first year after his wife walked out was "tough," a traumatic time when he grieved over the death of his marriage, the loss of someone he loved. He felt hurt pride, self-pity, and frustration as he tried to care for the needs of his small children and stay on top of his job. He missed his wife "terribly," but "the healing of a broken heart is helped by work of the hands to do. Keeping busy with my children has been a blessing."

What helped Harvey most was his belief in a loving God. "I felt that divorce was not his perfect will for my life, but I knew that he could bring good out of any circumstances if I allowed it. Daily and sometimes hourly prayer helped tremendously in handling negative emotions." Believing this, Harvey could choose not to retaliate against the one who had injured him, and "to allow her to control her own future."

Rebuilding is done in a context of other-centeredness. "Whoever loses his life for My sake, he is the one who will save it," said Jesus (Luke 9:24, NASB). We "lose" our lives for Jesus' sake by ministering to those in special need. "Inasmuch" as you feed the hungry, give drink to the thirsty, clothe the naked, and visit the prisoner, you do it "unto" Christ (Matthew 25:35-40).

Simply put: Find something to do for someone else. Move from preoccupation with your own loss to concern for someone else's need.

One Wednesday evening at our weekly church supper I sat beside a widow from Oklahoma who had come to visit her son, an officer in our church. She recalled her reaction to her husband's sudden death eight years before. "I went into depression and spent two weeks in a psychiatric unit. The doctors and my friends told me I must find something to do. After being home awhile, I went back to the very place where I had been a patient and got a job as a nurse's aide. I'm still there and having a wonderful time. You can't help others with their problems and worry about your own at the same time."

The tart-tongued "Miz" Lillian Carter of Plains, Georgia, is one of my favorite widows, although I grant she is not everyone's cup of tea. Miz Lillian is a trained nurse. To poor blacks in Plains with whom I spoke, she is a saint. Some say Miz Lillian provided the only medical care they could get for their children when discrimination reigned.

When husband Earl died, Miz Lillian's world, according to her daughter Ruth, "seemed to come apart." But not for long. She moved from Plains and took a job as housemother for a fraternity at Auburn University. "They made me feel young again." Then she took over a nursing home in Blakeley, Georgia, and tended to "old folks." Returning to Plains in 1961, she became restless and couldn't handle the widow's role people expected. She also felt a spiritual emptiness that could not be satisfied just by attending church.

One evening she accompanied daughter Ruth to hear a Methodist evangelist, Tommy Tyson. When he gave the call for "anyone willing to give up everything for Christ," Miz Lillian went to the altar and committed the rest of her life to Christ.

Back in Plains, she became angry with her church when the majority voted to exclude Blacks from services. One night, sitting up late mulling over her future, she happened to see a television commercial for the Peace Corps. Before going to bed, she wrote a letter offering to serve. The next morning she told her son Jimmy, not knowing how he would respond. "Mother, if that's what you want to do," he said, "then I'm all for it."

At an age when many women were retiring to

their knitting, Miz Lillian went happily off to India to work with lepers and help in birth control programs.

Eleanor Page joined Campus Crusade for Christ after her military officer husband died. The comely widow started a Bible study for women in the home of Mrs. John Conlan, whose husband was then a congressman from Arizona. Composed of wives and daughters of high government officials, the group grew rapidly and had to be divided. Among those who made professions of faith under Eleanor's teachings were the daughter of then President Nixon (Julie Nixon Eisenhower) and the wife of a high White House aide in the Nixon administration. These Bible studies sparked others, including one started by Eleanor in the White House for wives of administration employees.

In our travels to research missionary books, Marti and I have met many vibrant widows and widowers, some past eighty, in places where once only a David Livingstone would venture. We came upon Mrs. Duncan far back in the Peruvian jungle, typing the manuscript for the translation of the Campa Indian New Testament, done by her daughter and son-in-law, Mr. and Mrs. Lee Kindberg. As monkeys played in a banana tree outside their house, this silver-haired widow worked on the project. "My dear husband died last year," she noted when she stopped for coffee with us and her family. "I decided that instead of sitting around feeling sorry for myself, I'd just start out on a missionary career. The kids needed some help, so here I am. It's the greatest thing I've ever done, and I get to be with my grandchildren, too."

"Re-tired" and "re-cycled" widows and widowers scoff at danger in remote places within the sounds of native drums. "I'm a lot safer here than living in a big American city," more than one has told me.

I have to agree. ("The worst time," a retired teacher in Chicago said, "is the third of the month. That's when the criminals know we get our Social Security checks.")

It was a little riskier in Vietnam where widowed Leon Griswold went in the mid-1960s to help Christian & Missionary Alliance missionaries. In his youth, Leon had planned to be a career missionary. But business commitments and a growing family kept him home and he told his daughter Carolyn, when she departed for Vietnam, "You go in our place. Maybe someday we'll visit you on the field."

The years passed. Mrs. Griswold suffered a stroke and died before Carolyn could reach her bedside. Carolyn stayed home a few weeks to be with her dad, now a retired accountant. Just before she left, he said, "Do you suppose I could help you missionaries with your business affairs? There isn't much left for me here." Carolyn urged him to apply to their mission board for short-term service.

Leon was accepted and arrived in April, 1966, to live with Carolyn at the jungle highland town of Ban Me Thuot where the Alliance church had a Bible school and a leprosy clinic.

He was there in late January, 1968, when the Communists launched their bloodiest offensive of the war. Invaders charged across the Ban Me Thuot compound at 3:30 A.M., not sparing the missionaries. Bombs blew the houses apart. Carolyn was pulled from the wreckage of her house in critical condition. She lived only four days. Her father was found later buried under rubble. Four other missionaries were killed and two captured during the raid.

Four months after the massacre I walked through the ruins of what had once been the Griswolds' home. Vietnamese workmen were lovingly putting the finishing touches on a monument to the slain missionaries. I thought of Leon Griswold who had served only twenty-one months in his "retirement." Surviving missionaries said he had enjoyed every minute of it. Not one ever recalled hearing a word of self-pity from this man who chose to "lose" the rest of his life for Christ's sake.

A good marriage is a merging of personalities. Some couples can, after many years, come to look almost alike. When parting comes, the spouse that remains may have difficulty building a new life.

Whether you travel across the ocean, teach a Sunday school class, or serve as a volunteer in a mental health center, helping others after the loss of a spouse will help you build your identity as a single.

A widow who has submerged her interests to her husband's career may feel "lost,' unable to make independent decisions. This is why family counselors implore husbands to make their wives aware of business and financial affairs while both are living. Both spouses should know where wills, property deeds, bank books, and other vital documents are kept. Both should know how to balance a checkbook, file an income tax return, and dispose of property. It is even more important that each spouse maintain a psychological identity of his or her own.

All this advice may come too late for you. What if you failed to prepare for a single life? Don't despair. Building a new identity and role may be hard, but it can still be done.

Willie Jo Scott's husband Carl served as pastor of one church in New Mexico for twenty-five years. Then he died without warning on the day after Thanksgiving. The one she had loved above all else for forty-two years was gone—"the one," she said, "who had given me identity."

Willie Jo had worked and postponed having

children so her husband could get a ministerial education. After he became a pastor she "never scheduled a shopping trip, a visit home, a lunch with friends without first checking the church calendar to be sure there was no conflict. I worked in the church in every capacity a woman could. I began teaching public school only when our daughters started college.

"I was Mrs. Carl Scott, wife of the pastor. And nothing ever came before that." So when Carl died and she had to move out of the parsonage, she becme, in her own words, "Nobody."

While struggling in this limbo, Willie Jo heard about Charles Colson's Prison Fellowship. She wrote Colson, describing her predicament, offering to help. "I have been thinking a lot about the verse, 'If a man loses his life for my sake...'" she said. "I believe I feel what an inmate feels because I know what it is to be reduced to nothing. If there is any place of service for me with people in prison, I am ready."

Colson forwarded her letter to the Prison Fellowship representative in New Mexico. He gave her plenty to do.

She now helps with prison seminars as a volunteer and instructor. She visits inmates and corresponds with ten regularly. She keeps a long prayer list. Recently she gave Prison Fellowship a duplex home she and Carl had owned. Willie Jo Scott has found herself by losing her life in service for others. "Prison ministry is my place," she says.

Those who have become their own person after loss of a spouse often confess to having had feelings akin to guilt. To quote Cathy Kammas: "I feel most like I'm desecrating the memory of Pete when I say, 'I wonder if he'd understand me if he came back today?' I feel like I've grown so much. I've taken a business course and found my niche as an executive secretary—quite a role for a grandmother of seven!"

"When you lose your husband," Nadine Kaiser of Weatherford, Oklahoma, wrote in *Mature Living* (January 1982), "you can either die, too, or you can pick up the pieces and go on with what you have left." Nadine finds support to go on with four close friends, all widows, all retired from the Weatherford, Oklahoma, school system.

After their husbands died, the five banded together for companionship and mutual aid. Bernice's bathroom needed wallpapering. She didn't know how to do it herself, and she feared it would be too costly to hire someone. Her friend Olene proposed that if Bernice would buy the paper, she'd help her put it up. The next project was painting Olene's fence. A photographer for the local newspaper just happened to pass by while the widows were working. When the story appeared on the front page, calls began coming for "professional" work. The widows declined gracefully, saying this was not their intention at all.

All five have grown children, but none live close by. So while the widows don't live together, they have formed their own "family." Says Olene: "If one of us calls, and feels she's having one of her 'down' days, we get together. We've been good for one another."

In good weather, they walk together for exercise. During long winter months, they help each other with needlework. They belong to a travel club and have been to Europe several times. They're active in their respective churches.

The Weatherford Five are not a closed clique. They help shut-ins and others who need air and cheering up.

It's normal for people with common interests and needs to share work and concerns. If you're a widow or widower around fifty or over, the best place to find companionship may be in church. I've noticed that the widows in our church support one another with prayer and encouragement. But none are younger than fifty.

If you're a younger single, you may be disappointed, especially in a smaller church. You may feel like the proverbial square peg in a round hole.

If you're divorced, you would meet with some abrasion. Says George Ensorth, Jr., Professor of Pastoral Theology at Gordon-Conwell Theological Seminary: "More often than not, the church offers no support for the person caught in the painful grief of a living death: divorce. Divorce is a statement of failure not only for the persons divorcing, but also for the Christian church."

Dr. Ensworth speaks sadly of an active member of an evangelical church who was reeling from a divorce and the loss of his job. "He told me he could count on the fingers of one hand the people in the church from whom he felt real support. Others, he said, would turn down another aisle to avoid him as he entered the church. Some would admonish him to pray more, or to get his life in order so that God would bless his marriage and restore him to a job" (*Christianity Today*, May 21, 1982).

If you're worried about how you will be regarded, have a candid talk with the pastor. Learn how your church interprets the biblical passages on divorce. Honest Christians do differ. And there is not necessarily unanimity within denominations.

Ask if church policies prohibit divorced persons from holding church offices or teaching. You might spare yourself future humiliation.

Some churches and pastors allow no grounds for divorce. Some accept divorce as preferable to an unhappy marriage. A Gallup Poll for *Christianity Today* showed that about two thirds of U.S. pastors fall somewhere between these two extremes.

Clergy divorce is becoming more prevalent. The Reverend Lyle Schaller of Richmond, Indiana, a widely known researcher and interpreter of change in religious life, says there is now greater acceptance of clergy divorce than twenty years ago. He estimates that divorce will strike nearly 25 percent of clergy marriages, about half the rate among lay people.

Still, divorce for a clergyman can be devastating. Howard left a successful business career to enter the ministry. His wife did not feel "called" and inwardly rebelled. Just when Howard's first church was getting ready to "take off," his wife ran away with one of Howard's close deacon friends. Howard was distraught and devastated. "I wanted to die," he confided to me. "I flung myself before the pulpit, face-down, and cried and prayed all night. That Sunday I told my congregation that my marriage was over and asked for their prayers. They rallied around me and I survived."

The deacon returned and begged Howard's forgiveness. The wife vanished from sight. Howard remarried. Now, a quarter century later, he has a supportive, loyal spouse and a talented son and daughter. His son is his assistant pastor.

Howard's church grew to become one of the largest in his state. Occasionally I still hear someone—usually another minister—speak of him as "that divorced preacher," spoken from jealousy, no doubt.

That was twenty-five years ago. The pendulum has swung too far, I think, in acceptance of clergy divorce.

The names of two well-known Christian celebrities who recently divorced immediately come to mind. One has been the best known Christian writer on relationship theology for over two decades. He and his new wife are now writing books together. Another has been a popular writer on biblical prophecy. His "ministry" does not seem to have been affected, perhaps because his publishers have not publicized his divorce.

A third celebrity, who headed a multimillion-dollar Christian organization, recently stepped aside. His marriage is reported to be in serious trouble. This is not to mention a number of leading pastors whose marriages have collapsed. Nor the nationally known evangelist whom I cited earlier.

The positive side of this is that Christian leaders are less judgmental and more compassionate about divorce than in previous years. Perhaps some of us fear we could be next, although I cannot conceive of it in my own marriage.

The negative side is that the marriage commitment is not held as strongly among Christians as once was the case.

If you are a divorced Christian, striving to find fellowship and acceptance in a church, be aware of the dilemma in which many Christians feel caught. We want to help our divorced brothers and sisters begin rebuilding their lives. At the same time, we do not want to leave the impression that divorce is no different from changing one's address.

Of course, the widowed are under no stigma. Widows in the Old Testament were placed under God's special care (Psalm 68:5; 146:9; Proverbs 15:25). They wore a distinctive garb and were to be treated with kindness and respect. Anyone caught mistreating a widow was severely punished (Exodus 22:22; Deuteronomy 14:29; Isaiah 1:17; Jeremiah 7:6).

The first deacons of the early church were appointed to look after poor widows (Acts 6:1). Paul instructed Timothy to "honor" widows over sixty and see that they were provided for by the church (1 Timothy 5:3, 9, 10). Younger widows were not seen as in need of charity. It was felt that they could remarry (1 Timothy 5:11).

Paul does not mention widowers. He probably assumed they could take care of themselves. But an older Christian widow in the first century, without children or supportive family, had nowhere to turn but to the church.

Public welfare was unheard of then. Help is available from government sources today, but in our present tight economy it is becoming harder to get. Thankfully, churches are showing concern. Don't be too proud to ask your church for help. Some churches have special staff persons who can put you in touch with available resources.

Be warned that swindlers see a new widow or divorcee as easy game. Some watch the obituary columns to get prospects. Professional con artists know how to prey on your loneliness and vulnerability. When in doubt, check the person out. Stick close to trusted friends. Don't listen to strangers, especially to those who offer financial deals.

If you find yourself suddenly single, you'll be in special need of emotional support. Caring people who have walked where you now walk will understand. Despite what I've already said, do look first in your church. If it's a fairly large congregation, you may be surprised at the opportunities for fellowship with other singles. Some large churches will have a minister assigned to single ministries.

Still, most church programs are pitched to families. Being single can be more of a problem than being divorced or widowed. By default, many churches have said to singles, "We care only for couples and families."

Dr. Ruth Jacobs tells of Thelma, fifty-three and newly divorced. She moved to a new community and a new job to escape painful memories. The first Sunday, she attended the church of her denomination. Her hopes rose when a couple invited her to the coffee hour in the parsonage. Yet no one else spoke to her.

While everyone stood around chatting, she looked at the list of church organizations in a directory—a couples' club, a youth group, a senior citizens' group, and a ladies' auxiliary which met during her working hours. "I don't belong anywhere," she suddenly realized and rushed out before anyone could see the tears in her eyes. But she did put her name and address in the guest book. Months later she got a letter from the church, announcing the annual budget drive and including an envelope for her pledge.

Thelma tried a different church which advertised a Saturday night dinner and program for "special singles over thirty-five." These turned out to be special singles indeed, all patients from a mental health center.

Often the problem is with the demographic makeup of the community. Our town has few apartments. Most of the singles in our church are older widows. I've noticed that an occasional single career person drifts in from time to time. For awhile, a group of four or five tried having their own Sunday school class. They called themselves—appropriately—"The Misfits."

For several Sundays in a row I noticed Bridget, a recently widowed middle-aged neighbor, missing from her regular pew. She and her late husband had been pillars in the church. Their children had grown up in the Sunday school. I saw her one day in a store and asked if she had been sick or out of town. "Oh, I'm fine," she smiled. "I'm attending a downtown church. They have a marvelous singles' group." A year later I heard that Bridget had married a man she had met in the downtown group.

There are emotional advantages in moving to a new town, getting a new job, and forming new associations. Even without children, this may not be as easy as it sounds. Make sure you can get a job comparable to your present one before you sell your house. Before you make a clean break, decide if you can afford buying or renting in the new area.

What if you have school-age children? Bereft of one parent, they will need continued support from childhood friends, relatives, and familiar surroundings. Ann's husband died of a heart attack in his mid-forties, leaving her with children ages nine, eleven, and thirteen. Mortgage insurance paid off her house note. She wanted to move. She felt Jim's presence in every room and could not bear to enter his workshop off the garage.

Her childless married sister in another state kept begging her to move there. But every time she started to call a realtor, she thought of her children. Moving would uproot them from school, church, and a lifetime of friends. She also thought of her own links to the community. She would have only her sister and brother-in-law at the new location and would have to start over. Ann has elected to tough it out, at least until all the children are through high school.

Rebuilding your life will also involve a healthy sexual adjustment. By silence, the church has tended to deny that the formerly married have sexual needs. Society goes to the opposite extreme and assumes that the newly single is dying to jump into bed with the opposite sex. Thus the labels, "swinging single," "merry widow," and "gay (before 1970) divorcee." The pendulum has now swung so far that the world now presupposes that if you're formerly married and not seeking sex, then you must have some underlying emotional or sexual problem.

Studies do show that more formerly marrieds are sexually promiscuous than never marrieds (and divorced persons more than the widowed). But not everybody is doing it. And doing it will not enhance your emotional health.

This sounds terribly glib. Somewhat like the pastor who advised the middle-aged divorced man to go home and take a cold shower. The fellow told a friend: "How can he understand the intensity of my problem when he'll go home tonight and crawl into bed with a warm body—his wife."

A woman who felt terribly guilty after a sexual encounter that occurred a year after the death of her husband, said: "I was starved for affection. And I was afraid I might lose him. As it turned out, he did disappear."

After losing your spouse you can become very vulnerable to a sexual relationship you may have cause to regret for the rest of your life. Especially if you're a Christian. Even non-Christian psychologists advise that you're heading into stormy emotional waters by violating a long-time, deeply held value system.

Thankfully, help is available for those formerly married who are trying to maintain a Christian value system. Jim Smoke's book, *Growing Through Divorce*, is one helpful source. Jim also conducts some excellent seminars. The best book I've seen on coping with sex after divorce is Harold Ivan Smith's *A part of Me Is Missing* (Harvest House Publishers, Irvine, California 92714).

Now to the question most often asked by formerly marrieds: Will the rest of my life include remarriage? For most, the answer is eventually, "Yes."

The younger you are the better your chances. Your opportunities are also greater if you're a man. By age sixty-five there are 143 women in the U.S. for every 100 men. Widows account for 69.7 percent of all women over seventy. The older the eligible widower, the more he is sought after.

When we were visiting a retirement center in Florida, a seventyish widow pointed to a table beside the main door to the dining room. "That's the widowers' table," she grinned. "It's there so all the widows can look them over."

Age is no reason not to remarry. Having lost his beloved wife of fifty-eight years, the intrepid Lowell Thomas remarried at eighty-five and enjoyed four good years until dying at eighty-nine. Arthur Reed, who is 121 according to Social Security records has three marriages behind him and would like to marry again. "I don't want no old woman," the retired Oakland, California, carpenter said with a gleam in his eye. "Not over thirty-five. A woman of 125 couldn't get me a drink of water."

Marriages of persons past seventy appear to fare better than younger linkages. In 1970 Professor Walter C. McKain and associates of the University of Connecticut studied a hundred such marriages. They found only six failures, compared to thirty-three divorces for every hundred marriages then occurring. Seventy-four of the hundred older couples called their matrimony "highly successful."

Whether you're forty or eighty, man or woman, your biggest challenge may be finding good prospects. Chances are probably pretty small that you'll run into your old high school sweetheart, although it has happened.

Grace Jorgenson and Virgil Popejoy of Radcliffe, Iowa, broke up and didn't rediscover each other again for sixty-five years. Then Mrs. Jorgenson, a widow, heard that Mr. Popejoy's wife had died and she sent him a note of condolence. More correspondence led to a date at the altar.

Leck and Lucille were steadies at Central High School in Chattanooga where he was then the star football player. They graduated in 1933 and Leck went on to college and out of Lucille's life. Forty-seven years later, Lucille, who had moved to Florida and lost her husband, was visiting back in Chattanooga. She saw a newspaper picture of a group at an old timer's picnic and thought one looked like Lester Crew. "Could he be living here?" she wondered. She looked in the phone book and there was his number. After they got together again, Leck "took one look at her and all those old feelings started coming back." They were married five months later.

If you don't have an old high school sweetheart

LIFE CHANGES

waiting around, where are you to look? The logical answer is to go where the "fish" are. That's what Bridget, the middle-aged widow in our community, did. She quickly saw there were no "fish" in our church and went to another where there were.

Get out and mingle. Let people know you're single. You may find courtship the second time around to be awkward, frustrating, and painful. A man may find the "girls" more independent than those he dated in his adolescence. He may meet women who think if a man isn't interested in sex after one or two dates, then he must have a "problem." A woman may find men to be embarrassingly straightforward about sex, and vice versa. As a disillusioned woman told counselor Harold Ivan Smith, "Most of the time they give you three dates to go to bed. If you don't, they stop calling."

Sexual pressures have never been more intense and "Playboy" propaganda never more pervasive and beguiling than today. Yet with God's help you can take your stand pleasantly and firmly and hold your self-respect before friends and God.

It isn't necessary to frequent such sex flea markets as singles' bars. There are plenty of other places to meet eligibles—church events for singles, Christian conferences and retreats, political campaigns, civic projects, alumni gatherings, class reunions, Parents Without Partners, and ye old office, to mention a few. Get out and circulate.

Peggy Poor recalled to me how she met her new husband. "My church didn't have a singles department. After my husband died, I felt like a fifth wheel. Everything revolved around families. A divorced woman friend asked me to go with her to a local Parents Without Partners' meeting. She was too timid to go alone. The Lord must have planned it, for that's where I met Jim Poor, this beautiful man to whom I am now married."

George, a retired military officer, was not so

positive about his new wife when I last saw him. Widowed two years, George had recently married a never-married woman about ten years his junior. "I didn't know Marge as well as I thought," he confessed. "She has turned out to be stubbornly independent, and is trying to make me over in her mold. My advice to a widower my age contemplating remarriage is, 'Don't.' "

From what I know of George, he is pretty independent himself. His first wife was the type who let him make all the big decisions. His new bride isn't that kind. Somewhere, somehow, they'll have to make some compromises, or the marriage of two brittle people pulling against each other will inevitably break.

Rex, the widower left with three young children (whom I mentioned at the start of this chapter), was weary of single life when he met Helen, a never-married woman with great musical talent.

"When I saw this beautiful singer, I liked her immediately, and I could tell she liked me. When we did get married, people said we were made for each other. I was too blind, and anxious to remarry, to recognize what I was getting into. Our marriage was toxic from the start; but because we were both church workers, we stayed together. We sang together in churches and at Christian conferences and even made a couple of sacred records. People who saw us together assumed a beautiful relationship while we were hurting inside. We had a basic incompatibility that we never could work out."

Rex and Helen divorced after twenty-one years. He has since married again, this time to a divorcee with two minor children. "I was wiser this time and more mature," he reported.

Rex passed on this warning: "A widower with small children can remarry too fast for reasons which may seem valid at the time, but which later turn out to be wrong. Get to know the person well. Don't take things for granted."

For what it's worth: statistics show that second marriages of widowed individuals are more likely to last than those of divorced persons.

But don't let the mistakes and heartbreaks of others blind you from the fact that love can truly be wonderful the second time around. Cameron Townsend lost his first wife, Elvira, when he was forty-eight and general director of the fast-growing Wycliffe Bible Translators. After a time of bereavement, Cam's heart turned to Elaine Mielke, a Wycliffe missionary twenty years his junior. They enjoyed thirty-six marvelous years together and produced four wonderful kids before Cam died at eighty-five from acute leukemia.

Marti and I were privileged to write the biography of Cameron Townsend (*Uncle Cam*, Mott Media, Milford, Michigan). Cam and Elaine were one of the closest and most loving couples I ever knew. They were one in purpose to recruit more missionary translators for Bibleless language minorities. They delighted in doing things for one another. Cam enjoyed rising early to prepare breakfast. Elaine was always looking out for his welfare.

I was in their home a few days before Cam died. Home from the hospital, he sat weakly in his favorite stuffed chair with a covering lovingly tucked over his legs by Elaine. His throat had hemorrhaged the night before and he could not speak. But whenever Elaine came near, his eyes twinkled and he grinned like a sixteen-year-old seeing his first date. They were sweethearts to the end.

I saw Elaine eight months after Cam's death. Her ninety-one-year-old mother who had lived with her and Cam for many years had recently died, giving her a double loss. Yet she could talk about both with perfect aplomb. "Won't heaven be wonderful," she said. "I can hardly wait to see my dear Cameron and Mother again—and, just think, they'll be in perfect health."

Marriage can be great the first time, the second time, and every time for committed Christians.

The most famous widows in the evangelical Christian world during the past twenty-five years are undoubtedly the wives of the five missionaries killed by Auca Indians in Ecuador in 1956. The last book Marti and I did together was about the Auca experience and what had happened since the massacre (*Unstilled Voices*, Christian Herald Books, Chappaqua, New York).

Four of the five widows chose to remarry. One of the four was widowed a second time and is now married to her third husband. There is space here to tell only about two of the four, Marj Saint and Elisabeth Elliot.

Marj, the wife of martyred pilot Nate Saint and the one who kept contact with the five by radio before the killings, married Abe Van der Puy, then director of missionary radio station HCJB in Quito, Ecuador. Long before the violence on Palm beach, the Saints and Van der Puys were close friends. The Saint kids and the Van der Puy children had been schoolmates at the Alliance Academy in Quito. After Nate's death, "Uncle Abe," as the Saints called him, took them on fishing trips with his own children. Then Abe's beloved Dolores succumbed to cancer, leaving him to father their three alone.

Marj's friends were always wondering if she would remarry. Her Steve and Kathy, who had gone away to school, wrote her, "You don't ever need to get married. We'll always take care of you." But when they learned that Abe had proposed to their mother, they were overjoyed. "If it's Uncle Abe," Steve wrote, "that's different. When is the date?" Everyone who knew the Van der Puys and the Saints said the marriage would be like bringing six brothers and sisters together under the same roof.

So Marj and Abe were married on August 25, 1966, some ten and a half years after Nate's death, before

800 guests on the HCJB compound. Kathy Saint was her mother's maid of honor. Lois Van der Puy sang. Mark Van der Puy "stood up" for his father. Steve and Phil Saint and Joe Van der Puy ushered.

When the wedding photos were developed, Marj sent a pictorial story of the wedding to friends and relatives. "We're having a delightful time together as a family," she wrote. "All eight of us desire that the Lord use our lives and our home for his honor." The letter was signed, "Happy as can be, Abe and Marj."

And so it has been for all the years since.

Elisabeth Elliot has been twice widowed. After living with the very Indians who killed her first husband, Jim, Elisabeth and her daughter Valerie moved to the U.S. where she began a distinguished career as a writer and speaker. Elisabeth subsequently married Addison Leitch, a theologian, who died of cancer in 1974. It was "a gradual disintegration," she told me as we sipped coffee in her living room in a Boston suburb.

After Addison's death, she decided to take in student boarders from nearby Gordon-Conwell Theological Seminary, where Addison had taught and she served as a visiting professor of missions. One of the first two became her son-in-law, now a Presbyterian minister; the second, her third husband, Lars Gren.

I noticed that Jim Elliot's picture still hung on a wall. Mementos of Addison were still in the house. "I continue to use Jim Elliot's name on books and in public appearances, for that's what people know and remember me by," she said. "Both he and Addison still seem real to me." Remarriage doesn't wipe out your old memories. "But in private life," Elisabeth assured me, "I am very much 'Mrs. Lars Gren.' Lars is my manager and agent, travels with me, and handles the sales of my books."

Elisabeth has often been asked how to cope with the loss of a loved one. She summed up her experiences in an article for *Christianity Today* (February 27, 1976).

1. I try to "be still and know that He is God." In the midst of all this hullabaloo we are commanded, "Be still." "Be still and know."
2. I try to give thanks.... I can thank God for the promise of His presence. I can thank Him that He is still in charge....
3. I try to refuse self-pity.... It is a death that has no resurrection, a sink-hole from which no rescuing hand can drag you because you have chosen to sink. It must be refused.
4. I accept my loneliness. When God takes a loved person from my life, it is in order to call me, in a new way, to Himself.
5. I offer my loneliness up to God.
6. I do something for somebody else. There is nothing like definite, overt action to overcome the inertia of grief.

These six counsels can help you, as they helped Elisabeth Elliot, face and conquer the rest of your life. Job, living arrangements, social relationships, and even remarriage are all secondary and will fall into place if you let God be your refuge, your guide, and your commander as you seek to walk in the light of his way.

Even after the death of a beloved spouse, or after divorce, the rest of your life can be beautiful and wonderfully fulfilling.

6

Early Retirement

One balmy January evening in Anchorage, Alaska (if fifteen degrees can be called balmy), a pastor took me to dinner. The preacher had been bragging about people retiring in Alaska. "There's a couple," he pointed out, leading me across the restaurant.

Jim and Sarah McCullough greeted us warmly. Their drawl indicated that they were from the South. "Alabama or Mississippi?" I ventured. "Alabama born and raised," Jim said.

"So, how'd you get to Alaska?"

"Military. I spent thirty years in the army, twenty-three as a helicopter pilot with a stretch in Vietnam. I was stationed up here when I retired at fifty-three. Sarah and I went back to Alabama and looked around. We decided to come back to Anchorage. She has a good job here with the Red Cross and I've started a new career with the transit company."

Having just arrived, my blood has not yet thickened. "Oh, the climate isn't bad," Jim assured. "I've seen fifty-five below in the Arctic. Anchorage is really one of Alaska's warm spots. You know, just this morning we were talking to Sarah's mother on the phone. She said, 'Why don't you come back to Alabama and get warm?' I told her, 'It's warmer up here today than where you are.'"

Later in the week I bumped into a gregarious Texas Baptist layman who had come with a group to hold lay renewals in Anchorage churches. Sporting a broad-brimmed cowboy hat and a gleaming "Lone Star" belt buckle, Jimmy Delahoussaye looked about fifty-five, but was actually sixty-one (as I later learned). "This is my ninety-sixth lay renewal in five years," he reported. "I'm having the time of my life."

I wondered how even a Texan, unless he owned some oil wells, could take so much time off. "I'm not rich," he laughed. "I took early retirement at fifty-nine-and-a-half. One of the best decisions I ever made. Now I'm serving the Lord in a new career."

Back in the Lower Forty-Eighth I dropped into the office of friendly Bob Martin in North Carolina, at the headquarters of the Jungle Aviation and Radio Service (JAARS), a subsidiary of Wycliffe Bible Translators. He had been on the phone and was ready to take a break. "I love this job," he said. "We buy for over 4,000 missionaries scattered from Indonesia to Africa in places where you can't readily call up a parts supply house. Today we've got a new radio going to New Guinea for one of our planes, a small computer to Colombia, and books to a school in Peru. That's just a few examples. Whatever the missionaries need, we try to find."

Bob draws an early retirement pension from Ford Motor Company and serves the missionaries for no salary. He worked for Ford for twenty-six years and was one of five purchasing agents in the giant auto company before stepping out at fifty-five.

"The first six months my wife and I were here, we thought we had died and gone to heaven," he laughed. "We've enjoyed every minute working with folks who love the Lord. Feel better than I've ever felt in my life. I tell people, 'I'm not retired, just recycled.'"

Jim McCullough, Jimmy Delahoussaye, and Bob Martin are just three among thousands of active, healthy men and women who have stepped out of bread-and-butter jobs and taken early retirement before the customary age of sixty-five and moved into new and exciting careers. Some have taken regular jobs, others have launched into a self-employment profession or business, and still others, like Jimmy Delahoussaye and Bob Martin, are serving without regard to remuneration.

Early retirement after twenty or thirty years in the military has been common for many years. By enlisting at seventeen or eighteen, many have been able to retire on half pay before forty. Some remain in uniform longer and retire with more pension, allowing more financial freedom in taking on a new career. My former college classmate Dallas Roscoe became an army officer through the ROTC program, went to seminary, then became a chaplain. After almost thirty years he retired and embarked on a new career as minister to senior adults at a large church in Chattanooga. Dallas has one of the finest senior adult church programs I've ever seen. "I love working with these folks," he told me recently. "They're keeping me young."

Another ex-chaplain friend, Lewie Miller, Jr., was a long-time collector of rare and old Bibles. Retiring as a lieutenant colonel, Lewie opened a Bible museum in Gatlinburg, Tennessee, at the gateway to the Smoky Mountains National Park. When the World's Fair came to nearby Knoxville, Lewie moved part of his collection to the Baptist Pavilion. Thousands of persons saw his exhibit and heard him lecture. Last I heard from Lewie, he was working on a "computerized Bible." Said Lewie: "This is going to be a marvelous aid to Bible students and translators. You can instantly call up a Bible verse, phrase, or word in any of a number of languages."

Early retirement is no longer restricted to career military people. Many labor contracts now allow workers to step out with a pension after a certain number of years on the job, regardless of age.

The economic pinch of the 1980s is also pushing a growing number of company, institutional, and government employees to offer special inducements for early retirement. A lump sum payment, in addition to the earned pension, is typically given. Recently, some 1,000 Polaroid employees—nearly a sixth of the company's work force in Cambridge, Massachusetts, accepted a proposal which enabled the company to reduce personnel and cut costs. The average age of the retiring Polaroid workers was fifty-four. In our area, the Dupont company gave an incentive bonus for plant workers who wished to quit early and save younger employees from being laid off. Dupont's bonus equaled one week's pay for each year of company service, plus regular pension and other company-paid lifetime benefits.

Other trends point to more career changes by workers in the future. Advances in health and life expectancy are extending working lifetimes. Service occupations are gaining over factory employment. Jobs in heavy industry such as steel and auto making are decreasing, while vocations in high tech fields such as electronics and computers are skyrocketing. And greater emphasis is being put on personal fulfillment and job satisfaction. Call it early retirement, career switching, or whatever—the landscape of working is changing.

Around forty-five is the age when most workers begin thinking seriously of early retirement. If you're now, say, fifty, and can retire at fifty-five, you have only five years for planning. Time to get moving.

Start by checking the potential of your Social Security. Although you won't be eligible (unless you're disabled) until sixty-two, you need some idea of what to expect. Your Social Security office will provide a print-out of your earning record and Social Security contributions.

Suppose you have an IRA. You can't draw on it without a tax penalty for nine more years. With other investments which you control, you decide when to start paying yourself back.

Company or union pensions can be a thorny thicket. The 1974 Employee Retirement-Income Security Act requires companies participating in pension plans to make information available to their employees. But ERISA cannot make you understand the rules. You cannot afford to take anything for granted with a company or union-sponsored pension plan. Frank, for example, thought that since he had paid his union dues regularly he would certainly receive a pension. He didn't read the fine print about moving from one local to another with a different pension plan. When he went to get his pension after thirty-six years, he found he had nothing coming. Reason: Every local he had joined and paid into required ten consecutive years of employment for pension eligibility.

If you don't know your pension rights and guarantees from A to Z, get an appointment with your personnel director or employment counselor NOW. Find out if your pension is "vested"; if you leave before it is, you may lose all benefits. Vesting is based on various formulas. Most plans guarantee 100 percent of your pension eligibility after you have worked under a pension plan for ten years. Some, however, may provide only 50 percent vesting after five years of service, or even less.

Know the amount you will receive above Social Security at specific ages. Know your disability and survivor benefits. Know what will happen if your employer should go bankrupt or suddenly decide to get out of the pension plan.

As you get nearer your time of planned early retirement, you can be more specific in determining your assets. If you decide to sell your house and relocate, you will likely have a nest egg from the difference. Maintenance costs at your new location may be lesser or greater, depending on personal needs and support of dependents.

Subtract your projected living costs from anticipated income and you will know how much, if any, additional you will need to earn. This can also give you a guideline on how much you can afford to risk in a business venture.

Once you have a better picture of your finances, you can start considering the options open beyond early retirement.

Opportunities for adult education were presented in a previous chapter. Early retirement, especially if you have a monthly pension cushion, could give you the opportunity to finish the degree program you started or intended to start years ago. As already noted, you won't be the only one your age on a college campus. You might even find yourself attending with your children.

Ed Curry, after thirty years in the Air Force, enrolled at Cleveland State Community College in Cleveland, Tennessee. Taking night classes while holding down a full-time security guard job, Ed supported his family and earned an associate degree in Industrial Technology and General Business. "I had a ball," he said. "I enjoyed every minute of my college days." The postscript is that while Ed was studying, four of his children enrolled in the same school.

John Buckner took earlier retirement from the ministry to receive a pension from his denomination at sixty-two. The Reverend John promptly went back to college to earn a degree in history, while wife Juanita pursued her degree in library sciences. John took a post teaching history at the University of Central Arkansas, with Juanita becoming a high school teacher and librarian. John also continued preaching by serving a small rural church.

Most early retirees slide right into another job working for someone else. Unless you're going back to school for specialized training, it's advisable to have something lined up before you retire from your first career. It's always easier to get a new job while employed.

The sooner you start job hunting, the better. But take your time in filing for retirement. You're looking for something special and more fulfilling this time.

The temptation will be strong to take on something easy without a lot of pressure. Something that pays just enough to supplement your pension. You may enjoy this for awhile, but I predict you'll soon be bored and itching for a real challenge.

If you skipped chapter 3, since you aren't unemployed, go back and read the directions there for getting a good job. This chapter will emphasize opportunities for self-employment.

Who hasn't dreamed of being his or her own boss? Nobody looking over your shoulder. No time clock except your own. Set your schedule, work at your own pace, earn according to effort. It sounds so alluring. I have worked both for bosses and for myself. I much prefer the latter. But security is lacking, until you're comfortably established in your own business.

Not everyone is "cut out" to be his or her own boss. These check points from experts in vocational counseling might help you decide if self-employment should be in your future.

1. *Are you a self-starter?* Or does it take somebody else to get you going?

2. *Can you put yourself on a time schedule?* Or can you only work when you're in the mood?

3. *Can you stick with a job until it's finished?* Or do you turn to a diversion when a job becomes boring or hard?

4. *Can you make up your mind in a hurry?* Or do you need a lot of time to weigh all the pluses and minuses before you decide?

5. *Do you really like other people and can you get along with almost anybody?* Or do you cross the

street when you see someone coming who has rubbed you the wrong way?

6. *Are you the type who calls the tune, leads the way, and sets the pace when a job demands a group effort?* Or do you habitually hang back and wait for someone else to take command?

7. *Are you the kind who can be trusted to say what you mean and mean what you say?* Or do you tend to mumble ambiguities to keep from committing yourself to a difficult task?

8. *Are you the type who, when faced with a tough job, prays as if everything depends on God and works as if everything depends on you?* Or do you neither seek the Lord's help nor do your best?

If you answered the first questions (in italics) yes, chances are you have what it takes to be your own boss. You have initiative. You're a planner. You persevere. You make quick decisions. You have the basic component—liking others—for developing good interpersonal skills. You're a leader. You can handle responsibility. You're willing to pray fervently and work furiously.

If you're the second type in most instances, then you're more of a follower who requires disciplines and supervision from others. You probably wouldn't do well, nor would you be happy going on your own.

The most available self-employment is direct commission sales. In the bleakest depression, somebody is waiting to pay you a percentage for selling his products. When word gets around that you're retiring early, you may get a call like this: "Hey, Pal. I hear you're looking for a new career. Well, I've got something that's right up your alley. Howzabout me taking you to lunch and telling you all about it? Say, next Tuesday?" If you bite, the guy will try to sign you as a "distributor," "representative," "sales consultant," or with some other job title in direct selling. He may even provide you with some customer leads. But there'll be no guaranteed income and you might even lose a few bucks on your investment in a sample kit.

I'm not knocking direct selling. I worked much of my way through seminary selling appliances door to door in New Orleans on commission. This was during the early days of television. I would put two or three old black-and-white sets in my car, drive out into a residential neighborhood, and look for potential customers. I doubt if you could sell an antenna door-to-door today.

The TV commercials make it sound so easy to sell any line of goods. Some private distributors do make $100,000 a year and go to Hawaii and the Caribbean for sales conventions. Some cosmetic saleswomen do win pink Cadillacs for sales accomplishments. On the other hand, some don't average the minimum wage over a month's time.

Still, commission sales might be your key to prosperity and financial independence. If you're a guy or gal with drive, imagination, and a gift of gab, you can probably make more faster demonstrating and selling a good product than you could doing anything else.

I love selling, although I feel my calling is in religious communications (that involves selling, too). After working for the appliance store, I served as the young pastor of a little church for very low pay. One day I was calling on an entomologist friend, Bob, who ran a one-horse pest control business. He made service calls for five dollars a month, guaranteeing to keep a home free of pests. We made a deal. I would sell yearly contracts for him at 20 percent commission. He would do the dirty work.

I canvassed householders in a string of new housing developments, asking if they would be interested in subscribing to a community pest control service. Bob had agreed to knock a dollar off per visit, if I could line up a dozen or more customers within an area of a few blocks. If the customer was interested, I'd say, "Let me check with your neighbors and see if we can get enough stops for a reduced price." I did all the canvassing on weekdays, in between pastoral calls. Saturdays, I went back and signed people up by the score. By the time Orkin, our big competitor, got wise to what was happening, I had most of the market locked up.

I am by nature a high energy person. Some days I run on sheer enthusiasm. Direct selling is ready-made for people like me. But if you're a shy, low-energy person, who couldn't sell a refrigerator in a heat wave, then don't let yourself be talked into believing you could be a super direct salesman.

Franchising is a little different from commission selling, although the principle that you earn according to your skill and effort is the same. Franchising usually requires a sizable cash investment in equipment, a store, or a plant. You can invest thousands before you make the first sale.

You're safest with a proven producer and a known product. You take a bigger risk with an unknown. Don't be snowed by a fast-talking promoter from a franchiser you never heard of. Check everything. Talk with other franchises and not just the ones the promoter recommends. Get all the facts and take all the cautions before pitching in a bundle of your precious savings.

With direct commission sales, the most you can lose is your time and maybe a few dollars for samples. With a franchise backed by a good company, your risks are not great. You take the greatest risk when you move into unmapped territory and open your own business. Yet this is the way most great fortunes are made. It is also the way many well-intentioned entrepreneurs lose their shirts. Whether you lose it all or make a million could depend on how well you plan your operation.

My parents were poor dirt farmers in 1939. That year they moved from a literal wilderness to a house on an unpaved state highway. While Daddy tended to the crops, Mother sold groceries from a side room to neighbors. She liked this. She made a few dollars. A couple of years later they borrowed $350 and bought an empty grocery store in a small town. They never heard of a market survey, but they knew the people were there and the corner location was good. They did OK.

Today you can easily get expert advice from proven successes. Besides "how-I-did-it" books you'll find in your local library directories of resources for almost any type of business. A directory of trade associations will tell you where to write for basic information about the industry or trade in which you're interested. You can order for pennies from the Small Business Administration booklets on how to finance, start, and maintain a business. You can call on a field office of the SBA and stop in at the nearest Chamber of Commerce for personal advice. There's a lot of help out there, but you have to ask. Don't risk your stake on hunches, intuitions, and tips from well-meaning friends. Starting a business today is a little more complicated than what it was when my parents started selling groceries forty years ago.

Learn from George, who accepted a bonus offered by his plant for early retirement. Wife Margaret was already wallpapering for friends to earn extra money. "Why don't we open a paint and wallpaper store?" George said.

They were scouting for a location when a guy who had retired with George directed them to a small vacant building next to the big supermarket where he now worked. "We don't sell wallpaper," he assured. "You can catch some of our traffic."

George put his bonus money into fixtures and stock and signed a two-year lease. Business was great for three months. When the supermarket next door closed and relocated in a new shopping center a mile away,

George and Margaret's sales dropped 70 percent the next month. They tried every promotion gimmick they could think of. Nothing worked. Without the supermarket next door, they couldn't lure enough customers into the store. After four straight months of losses, they had to close and borrow money to settle up the lease balance.

They had hitched their wagon to traffic generated by the supermarket. If they had checked with the store manager, perhaps they might have learned of the proposed relocation before leasing the adjoining building.

Patricia Geffette of Seattle has a brighter story because she made careful preparations every step of the way.

When Patricia decided to go into the contracting business she had eighteen years of experience behind her in keeping books for a construction company, managing apartments, and testing soil samples on new building sites. She already knew her way around.

She started by locating two building lots for $24,000. Before putting any money down, she went to the City Planning, Building, and Public Works departments. She found the zoning classification and restrictions, availability of utilities, and improvement plans for the street. Then she bought the land.

Her next investment was in construction. She partly finished one house, put it on the market, and waited. When she got a buyer she finished that house and started another. Last I heard, this foresightful and enterprising lady had ten employees, with eleven houses and a sixteen-unit apartment-townhouse complex going up.

Guidelines for all businesses aren't the same. If you're going to sell by mail order from a post office box, location of your office may be irrelevant. If you're opening a bookstore, location can be everything.

Planning ahead is absolutely essential. If you

can test the waters before you leave your employer's nest, you might save yourself a bundle of risks and worries.

My fellow church member Leon Webb worked twenty-two years in television, advancing from engineer to operations manager of a Chattanooga station. Two years before leaving his television job, Leon bought a small press and did printing for friends at night and on weekends. "I wanted to see how well I liked printing and if I could build up a clientele and buy some equipment while I was still on salary," he said.

Leon succeeded on all counts and now has his own thriving printing business, handling customers all over this metro area and even shipping work out of state.

At thirty-three I retired from working for someone else, although I hadn't worked long enough to have a pension. Like Leon, I began laying the groundwork at least two years before resigning from a job with a regular paycheck. I wrote books and articles three and four evenings a week. When I was ready to launch out into the "deep," I had one royalty book selling in bookstores, two in the process of publication, and two more under contract. More important, I had built up a reservoir of editor contacts and potential assignments for the future.

A number of friends warned me that they didn't know anyone who had ever survived financially as a free-lance religion writer. Joe Bayly, the managing editor at the publishing house where I was an editor, hinted several times that I might be making a mistake. Finally, on my last day in the office, Joe said, "Well, I'll envy you thirteen out of every fourteen days. The fourteenth, you know, is when we get our paychecks."

Our oldest daughter was then only eight. I told her that her daddy would now be working at home. "But who will pay you money?" she asked astutely. Good question. I presented the possibilities of free-lance writing. Her puzzled face indicated that she wanted a more substantial answer. Marti held out my one book which was then selling in Christian bookstores for fifty cents. "For every one of these people buy, we will get a nickel." "A nickel!!" Cyndi frowned. "A nickel a book. We'll starve!"

We elected to stay in the Chicago area where most of my markets were located. O'Hare Field, the world's busiest airport, was nearby, affording quick and fast transportation to distant cities where I might be researching stories. This proved to be a sensible decision for the first few years. After I was well established, we moved to a more enjoyable living environment on a mountain in Tennessee.

I've been asked more times in writer's workshops than my IBM Selectric has keys for tips on making it as a self-employed writer. Boiled down to seven steps, what I tell them is applicable, I believe, to any profession in which you try to make it on your own.

1. *Start with what you know and develop other interests and talents gradually.* My first article sales were to publications which I had been reading and enjoying for years. I wrote about subjects which were familiar to me.

2. *Start small and work up.* A fellow came up to me at a writer's conference in California. "I'm very discouraged," he said. "Everything I've submitted has been rejected." "What markets have you been trying?" I asked. "Well, just the *Reader's Digest*. I thought it might be best to start at the top." I had to tell him that this was like an auto mechanic trying to start a repair job on a rocket booster. "Your chances are much better writing for magazines with small circulations," I suggested. "These editors will be glad to work with you if you have average talent. The pay isn't so great, but you can learn on the job."

3. *Do the best work you can.* For a writer this

means adequate research, accurate writing, and persistent rewriting until you believe an article or chapter is the very best you can produce within your limits of time and talent. The late Catherine Marshall was an excellent writer whose books continue to sell in the millions. She rewrote the first chapter of her best-selling novel *Christy* eighteen times.

4. *Take advice from editors.* Your friend or spouse may be not only unqualified, but unwilling to tell you the brutal truth. This does not always hold. My wife and I read each other's work regularly and offer suggestions for improvement. However, we do it in a businesslike way with no thought of putting the other down.

Editors, for a writer, are the judge and jury. My first articles brought detailed instructions from editors on how improvements could be made (at least they believed in me and my ideas). A tart-tongued woman editor once declared of a piece I sent her youth magazine, "How corny can you get?" I revised according to her directions and sold it. The article later became part of my first book.

5. *Keep learning.* I never had a college course in journalism and began writing professionally at twenty-six. Besides learning from editors, I took a beginner's correspondence course. I read every writing resource book on the shelves of the New Orleans Public Library and subscribed to *Writer's Digest,* the best trade magazine for a writer.

Every trade with more than a few thousand people in it has specialized literature. Use your library. Read the trade magazine. The information train in many fields is now moving almost at the speed of light. You can't afford to get behind.

6. *Be dependable.* Writing is one of the few trades left where verbal agreements are expected to be honored. This is for articles, however; books are

contracted. Contrary to popular opinion, an editor does not work with the most talented writers. He deals with the most dependable ones, a few of whom are very talented.

7. *Be available for emergencies.* The phone rings. "Can you do a piece for me fast? Have it in the mail day after tomorrow? The assigned writer missed his deadline." Or, "My managing editor threw out one of my selections at the last minute, and I've got to have a filler." Or, "Can you cover a late-breaking news story? Like tonight?"

During my early writing years, when I needed work worse than I do now, I put out a lot of fires. "Firemen" will always get work. Every customer has emergencies when he needs an essential product within hours or days. Business is given to the guy who says, "I'll have it on your desk no later than ———," and delivers.

I earn almost all of my living from writing. At times I long for the luxury of being able to write without regard to payment. There are some books I would like to do but simply cannot because the expected return will not justify the time required to do the job. "Someday," I keep telling myself.

Some fortunate persons reach that idyllic "someday" when they retire at fifty-five or earlier. Some choose to go on working for pay, even though a paycheck is not necessary for comfortable living. Some decide to devote the rest of their lives to volunteer work or some type of Christian ministry.

Millard Fuller became a millionaire before forty. Then he dedicated the rest of his life to helping the world's have-nots obtain decent housing.

Lem Clymer retired in 1978, in his mid-fifties, from the presidency of the world's largest motel chain, Holiday Inns. What precipitated his early retirement was the company's decision to build gambling casinos.

"When I considered the implications it became clear that I had come to a fork in the road. I decided to follow a different road, one which would leave more time available to serve the Lord. Now I consider myself so blessed by being able to work with my minister as an assistant for special projects. I have the opportunity of working with volunteers in evangelistic outreach, serving as chairman of our missions committee, and doing other volunteer work with civic organizations. The years since I retired have been the most rewarding of my life."

The New Testament teaches that *all* believers are ministers. Awareness of this revolutionary teaching has directed many early retirees into full-time Christian work after retirement. Typically, this is their testimony: "I once thought that ministers and other professionals were to do the spiritual work, while we laity were to usher, take up the collection, handle church finances, and maybe teach Sunday school. Now I know that the job of the professionals is to equip the whole body—all of us in the church—for the work of the ministry (Ephesians 4:12). God calls us laity to do the work of ministry for which we are trained."

Jimmy Delahoosaye discovered this radical truth when a lay renewal team came to his church in Texas. As Jimmy recalled to me, "A member of the team stood up and said: 'Write down whatever is standing between you and making a full commitment of your life to God.' I wrote down my job and laid the paper on the altar.

"Later that evening my blind, diabetic wife Margaret and I were praying together. She began asking the Lord to have his will in our lives. God convinced me right then that I should resign my job and serve full time in lay renewal. But I didn't yield. I argued with God that I couldn't make it.

"This went on for days and days. As I went

through my daily routine, I was the most miserable human being that ever lived. After an almost sleepless night I'd get up and give Margaret her insulin shot, fix her breakfast, and get off to the Texaco plant where I was assistant superintendent of manufacturing. All day, I'd argue with God and worry. Then I'd go home and hear Margaret tell me about her glorious day spent praying for people on the telephone. 'Hotline Delahoussaye,' they called her. People would call and she'd pray for them right on the spot. All the time she was praying for me, too, that I'd let the Lord have his way.

"On February 1, 1977, I made a commitment to quit work. I would be fifty-nine in three more years, and eligible for a pension. Until then we figured we could live off our savings. Six weeks later the plant blew up and killed sixteen people. One of the men killed was the man who took my place. I figured the Lord must have been looking out for me.

"We were just getting started in lay renewal when Margaret had to enter the hospital. Her forty-one-day stay took all our savings. The Lord provided a job as site manager at a sulphur mine in Louisiana. We planned that I would work there until the pension came due at fifty-nine.

"I was making pretty good money when Texaco notified me that my monthly retirement checks would begin. I wrestled with the idea of staying a few more years and putting a little extra money away. Finally, on April 28, 1980—a date I'll always remember—I came home at four in the afternoon and said, 'Honey, what am I working for?' She said, 'To be a millionaire, I guess.' I said, 'There's no way that will happen.' I went back, said my good-byes, cleaned out my desk, and we hit the road full time for the Lord."

Their first year Jimmy and Margaret participated in thirty-six lay renewals. Paying their own expenses, they traveled 63,000 miles. In July, 1981, they were at a church just outside Melbourne, Australia, for a weekend. On Saturday morning, Jimmy brought a man to faith in Christ. The next morning Margaret spoke in church; then the coordinator of the renewal group gave an invitation to publicly confess Christ. Jimmy's man was the first down the aisle; followed by his daughter, making a first-time profession; then his wife coming to renew her vows. "The Holy Spirit of God broke loose in that church," Jimmy recalled. "Twenty-five people came to Christ in one day."

While they were still in Australia, Margaret reentered a hospital for the last time. "We both knew that if I hadn't quit work we wouldn't have had a glorious year together serving the Lord full time," Jimmy said. "We just praised the Lord in that hospital room.

"A week later, on Sunday morning at one A.M., Margaret went into cardiac arrest. I had my thumb against her neck vein and felt the last heartbeat. The doctor reached out and pulled my hand away and said, 'Jim, she's with her Heavenly Father.' I felt no sorrow, I just said, 'Thank you, Lord, for taking her to where she'll have perfect sight.'"

It was about a year after Margaret's death when I saw Jimmy in Anchorage. He said he was going to remarry. "The Lord is giving me a lady I've known for thirty-two years. She's the widow of an old friend who used to ride to work with me. It turns out that our children are the same age—we each have three—and went to the same high school.

"Naturally," Jimmy said, "I intend to continue in lay renewal for as long as the Lord gives me strength to go. I will just have a new partner."

Bob Martin, the former Ford purchasing agent, didn't suddenly get interested in helping missionaries. Bob and Betty taught Sunday school for many years and Bob was a deacon in their church in Michigan. "This and being a Gideon," Bob said, "gave me a real interest in the

Bible." The Martins had first-hand contact with missionaries when they lived in South America for awhile, when Bob was with Ford. "The Lord had been preparing us for a long time," Bob said.

Buying for Wycliffe's far-flung corps of translators and support personnel is a tough and challenging job. "Hardest to get," Bob said, "are parts for outdated equipment such as Helio Courier planes which can land on short jungle air strips and which are no longer made." If there's a part available, Bob and his co-workers will find it. Often he finds himself calling upon suppliers he used to deal with when he was at Ford. "When they find they are dealing with a Christian organization they tend to hurry things along a bit. Some will give a discount when otherwise they would not."

From time to time Bob runs into old friends who "can't believe I am working for no salary. I tell them I get the best pay in the world in satisfaction that I'm helping our folks take the Word of God to Bibleless tribes."

Bob and Betty live in a community of about four hundred, some thirty miles south of Charlotte, North Carolina. All of their neighbors are involved with JAARS and Wycliffe. Some are full-time missionaries, serving at the JAARS headquarters or taking orientation for field assignments. Over half are retired folks, like the Martins, who live in their own homes or rented apartments and help as "associates."

The associates work in the post office, serve as radio operators sending and receiving messages to Wycliffe fields, repair airplanes, do plumbing and electrical jobs, work on roads, cook and serve in the dining hall, teach missionary children, and perform a host of other services which free the missionaries for their career assignments. Both husbands and wives are involved. While Bob Martin is purchasing supplies,

Betty Martin teaches sewing to newly appointed missionaries headed for jungle stations.

"We have plenty of work for early retirees here at JAARS," Bob reported. "When I got here they had an office and telephone waiting for me. Write to JAARS or Wycliffe. Tell us what you can do. Make yourself available. We'll find a job for you."*

Early retirees serving with other mission groups give the same advice. Opportunities await, including overseas assignments in which you will work side by side with career missionaries.

If you're retiring early, this is a great day to be alive. You have flexibility which you didn't have when you were starting out twenty or thirty years ago. You should have twenty to thirty good years ahead, depending upon your health. Whether you're taking a new job with another company, launching a business or trade, or signing up for full-time service to God and your fellowman, a challenging future lies before you. Start planning now so that when the time comes you are ready for takeoff into new horizons.

*Jungle Aviation and Radio Service, Box 248, Waxhaw, NC 28273; or Wycliffe Bible Translators, Huntington Beach, CA 92648.

7

Hanging It Up at Sixty-five

The university cafeteria was crowded. "May I sit with you?" the bearded professor asked.

"Well, well," he said when I told him I was researching retirement. "I'm retiring from the faculty shortly. My wife and I *know* what we're going to do. We're going to buy a sail boat in California and head out to sea."

"Where?" I wondered.

"To an island in the South Pacific we've been reading about."

"Sailing is your hobby, I suppose?"

"I haven't done too much. Just a little off the North Carolina coast."

"What will you do when you reach that island?"

"Oh, we'll stay there awhile."

"After that?"

"Oh, we'll move on to another place. Wherever the wind leads us."

Here was a doctor of philosophy, a veteran teacher and guide to thousands of students, whose retirement plans were frighteningly vague. He was taking his trusting wife to a place they had only read about. And he didn't know what they were going to do after that. About as bad as the retired plant executive in Tucson who told me, "I moved out here to fish and play golf. Retirement soon became a bore."

To "retire" is literally to "draw back," "fall

back," "withdraw." In military terms, to retire is to retreat. In baseball parlance you are "put out." In occupational usage, you "withdraw from your usual position or work."

"Retired" is frequently used in obituaries to describe the last status of a deceased person.

> John Gladewater, 67 of 1312 Orange Street, died in a local hospital Monday morning. He was a member of Union Grove Baptist Church, a veteran of World War II and a *retired* employee of U.S. Pipe Co. Arrangements will be announced by Franklin-Strickland Funeral Home.

You even see "retired farmer" in obituaries now. My granddaddies would have protested that word ever being used for them. Grandfather Hefley raised corn and cotton until he was felled by a stroke. Grandfather Foster kept working until he could no longer stand in the bean row.

Retirement is a child of the industrial age. A misbegotten child, many think. Feisty Dr. Joseph H. Peck dedicates his book *Let's Rejoin the Human Race* "to man—the beauty of the world, the paragon of the animals—due to be emasculated and driven from the kingdom at the age of sixty-five." Dr. Peck notes that retirement has produced a whole new economy. "There are more people doing research and writing about us oldsters than there are oldsters to write about.... How has all of this attention affected grandpa? Well, I can testify that if he tries to read half of what is written, he will wind up nutty as a pet coon."

Unless you're self-employed and can quit, slow down, work, play, or travel as your income permits, you have to live with the system. Sixty-five is the legal age for most employment. Some college professors, for example, can hang onto work a few years longer. A prof I know got an extension on his sixty-fifth birthday. He can't be booted out for five more years. Then he must retire.

As "Bear Bryant" said upon announcing he would coach only one more game: "There comes a time when you need to hang it up, and that time has come for me as head football coach at the University of Alabama."

Most workers like the professor I met in the cafeteria want to get out at sixty-five. You see the fateful time coming around the bend. The birthdays come rushing past faster and faster.

The big day arrives. The end of an era and the opening of a new book. The boss calls you in and gives you a little patter of appreciation. Your immediate co-workers gather around and the treasurer presents you with a plaque to hang in your den and a bonus for you and your wife to take a cruise or a trip to visit the grandchildren. Everybody applauds. Joe, the guy who always emcees the Christmas parties, cracks, "Well, it's been good working with you. Think of us poor slaves when you're teeing off the ninth hole in Miami or snagging a lunker on that Minnesota lake." Joe hands you a ribboned package he's been holding behind his back. "We all chipped in to give you this to remember us by." You unwrap the gift, thank everybody, shake hands all around, swallow a few lumps, and edge out the door awkwardly.

"Come back and see us," someone yells.

"Sure," you say, "I'll be around."

Whether you're the executive vice president or the custodian, the difference will be only in style and expense. If you're a big wheel you could get a dinner in your honor at the country club and an hour of tributes. But the feeling will be the same. Doug and Faith Mains, long-time owners and operators of an advertising agency in Wheaton, Illinois, recalled for me their last day at work. "You have the banquet and hear all the speeches," Doug remembered. "The time comes to walk out of the business you've sold and turned over to a younger person. You tell yourself, 'Well, here it is.' It's difficult, numbing. But you do what you're supposed to do and get into your car and drive away. You're gone for a week or two, then you go back for just a 'visit.' Everybody looks at you a little strangely. It's no longer the same."

Whatever the ceremony, gifts, and tributes, you're saying farewell. Good-bye to a long-established priority and piece of your life. Good-bye to regular association with people you may know better than some members of your own family. Good-bye to coffee breaks and office parties. The impact doesn't hit until the next Monday when you don't have to catch the 7:27 bus. You sleep late, then get up and tackle the chores you've been saving for yourself. The week wears well as you get your workshop in order, play a couple of rounds of golf, go bowling, and try the bass up on Cedar Lake. You keep thinking of the old gang. By the middle of the second week, you can't wait any longer. You stroll into the plant or office in the middle of the morning.

"How ya enjoyin' your freedom?" Joe asks.

You give everybody the glad hand, kid a lot, talk about the weather on the golf course and the big one that didn't get away. After a few minutes, you can tell your old associates are getting edgy. Then someone says, "Well, nice seeing you again." He means the work must go on without you. You get the message. You're out. Done. You'll see them again at the annual banquet, where you'll be recognized along with the other retirees. It won't be the same. It never will be. This part of your life is over. You're retired.

William Wilson is visitation pastor of a large church in Tucson. He counsels hundreds of retirees every year. "Many that I see here have no life purpose. Maybe they came to Tucson because they heard living is cheap.

It isn't. The 'snowbirds' come for the winter and go back North in the spring. Those who come to play and stay soon get tired of fun and games. They really don't know what they want. Many already have health problems when they retire. With time to sit around and think about their aches and fears, they get worse and end up in the hospital. We telephone their children who live in New York or Minnesota. Some of the kids just ask a few questions and hang up."

Joan Nielsen, a petite, pretty social worker for the elderly in Tucson, said loneliness was the biggest problem of most retirees she sees. "They leave their children and social contacts up North and come here not knowing a soul. I see people who never leave their home, except to go to the grocery and the doctor. They just let things happen. Some start drinking heavily. One day they run out of money and have no place to live. An upper-class housing development here brags about 'the grin of satisfaction' among their elderly residents. We social workers say 'the grin comes from drinking too much gin.' A study among the occupants showed the average household there consuming five quarts of liquor per week."

A tax-consultant in El Paso, another retiree haven, echoed what I heard in Tucson. "So many retire, thinking only, 'I'm tired and just want to rest.' Recently I asked a widower who was getting ready to retire what his plans were. 'I'm going fishing a lot with my friends.' 'Your friends,' I said. 'Do they work? Will they be able to get off every time you want to go fishing?' He hadn't thought of that."

Counselors and social workers say the divorce rate among people over sixty-five is astounding. A church secretary in El Paso told me her parents had recently separated after forty years of marriage and fourteen children.

Many retired couples are simply unable to

LIFE CHANGES

adjust. A typical man with a wife at home has been out of the house ten hours a day, five days a week for almost all of his marriage. Now he is home every day with no regular schedule. His wife gets sick of having him underfoot. He's too bossy and is trying to take over her domain. He eats when he feels like it and upsets her meal plans. Finally she blows her stack: "I never did tell you how to run your office. Now you quit telling me how to run the house." He slinks off to nurse his hurt feelings. The silences get longer.

Life expectancy may not be so good either. Dr. Sam Walters, a Kansas City, Kansas, nutritionist, noted that the average male at loose ends after retirement lives only 2.4 years. "He doesn't get enough exercise. He consumes more calories than he burns. He rides a mower instead of pushing it. He eats junk food because he has nothing better to do. He sits for hours before the TV. The fatty deposits build up in his liver and blood vessels. Before you know it, he's gone."

It isn't just the poor nutrition and lack of exercise. Dr. Peter J. Steincrohn warns retirees: "Chronic boredom is slow death."

Boredom settles in when life has no purpose or meaning. Like many, your self-esteem may have centered on your work. I'm haunted by what Dave Garroway, the first "Today" show host, told his former news colleague, Frank Blair: "I'm old shoe, old hat. Nobody cares for old Dave any more." Garroway then went out and shot himself. He was sixty-nine.

I asked about twenty Christian retirees in El Paso for advice, based on their experience, on what to do and not to do in retirement. Here's what they suggested:

Establish a regular devotional time; keep going to church; keep your life well organized; find a new hobby; keep on with night activities; stay active physically; be friendly; stay busy; travel some; take care of your health; enjoy your family more; and work as long as you can.

They warned against: becoming too dependent on others, being too sensitive, spending too much time alone or with TV, moving far away from home, losing your temper, eating too much, and interfering with the children.

What you accomplish and enjoy in your "golden" years depends largely on your attitude. Attitudes of the over-sixty-five are conditioned more by myths than reality. One bit of folklore says the ages of man are revealed by what he talks about. The young man tells about the date he had last night. The forty-to-sixty-year-old describes the grand dinner he had yesterday. The man over sixty brags about a successful trip to the bathroom this morning.

The most common myth is that you're "over the hill" at sixty-five. Older people do go to the doctor more often than younger persons. But people over sixty-five, according to medical writer Bernice Hunt, have only about half as many acute illnesses as young sprouts age seventeen to forty-four.

Your math I.Q. does go down as you get older, observes Pennsylvania psychiatrist Dr. Aaron Beck, but your verbal I.Q. tends to go up. On the average, at sixty-five you can expect to live sixteen more years, and longer if you pursue a sensible life style.

Attitudes influence your health. As you think, so are you (Proverbs 23:7). If you "think" you have a serious problem, get an expert medical opinion instead of brooding. If tests do show a real ailment, have it treated and quit worrying. Adopt the theme song of the old-time Carter family: "Keep on the Sunny Side of Life." Practice Norman Vincent Peale's "positive imaging." Tell yourself, "Every day in every way I'm getting better and better." Tone up your muscles and build up your cardiovascular system with exercise. Slim down your body and pep up your energy with good nutrition. Shape up and feel twenty years younger. You're not in the hearse by a long shot.

"Through your life style," says Dr. Donald M. Vickery, "you control your health more than your doctor does." If you don't believe this is true, take one of those "lifescore" tests that frequently appears in magazines and newspapers. You may be surprised at what you can do to increase your score.

Give yourself a top-to-bottom financial check-up. Ideas on what you should cover were outlined in the chapter on early retirement. But this one should be more detailed. You have fewer financial options at sixty-five or seventy, than you had at fifty.

Draw two columns on a single sheet of paper. Title the first column Assets, and list your home, other real estate, furnishings and car, checking and savings, stocks and bonds, retirement accounts such as I.R.A. and annuities, and any amounts you are owed. Under Liabilities, put down credit cards, installment accounts, personal loans, etc. Subtract liabilities from assets and you've got your net worth. If retirement is, say, five years in the future, try to project what your new worth will be at that time. Simple. But it's surprising how many people come up to retirement without knowing how much they're worth.

Take another sheet and two more columns. Head the first column Projected Monthly Income (or just "Income" if you're already retired). Put down Social Security, pension, interest, dividends, rents, etc. Under the second column, Expenses, note what it takes (or will take) to maintain your desired life style—house mortgage, taxes, food, clothes, utilities, recreation, transportation, church gifts, home repairs, etc. This is nothing more than a budget which you may have been operating under for years. The difference is that your retirement income will be less, possibly much less. And except for Social Security, your intake will probably be "fixed," while your expenses will keep going up because of inflation. This may require selling some property and/or moving to cheaper living quarters.

Income reduction at retirement can be a shock, a heavy blow, unless you prepare ahead of time. Norman and Ruth Hodges avoided this shock by starting on his sixtieth birthday to begin living on the budget projected as equal to the one they would have on retirement. They put the difference between his income and projected retirement expenses into repairing and replacing essential items needed during retirement and into a savings program.

Prudent money management is closely linked to the decision of where to live. Many retirees in different living situations told me that this was their most difficult decision. Some admitted that they had made their greatest mistake by making a sudden move without proper preparation.

You will not be entirely "footloose and fancy free" even if money is no object. During your lifetime, you've established precious ties and relationships with loved ones, friends, church, and other stabilizers which give you a secure "place" in the world. Extended travel will probably create no strain, for you will be returning to the "old stomping ground." Absence from familiar faces and places will make your heart grow fonder. Friends and loved ones mean more as we get older.

Every retiree I talked to about moving advised, "Go slow. Don't make any quick decisions. Test the water. If possible, try a new situation before you move, especially if it's far away from the old hearth."

Doug and Faith Mains first spend several winter vacations in Boca Raton, Florida. "By the time we decided to buy a condo, we had already found a church and friends," Faith said. John and Marie Fouse, also from

Illinois, made at least ten trips to Arizona before buying a house, settling down in a dry, warm climate, and becoming involved in a church they've "learned to love."

You could simply stay where you are, especially if the climate presents no problem to your health. Bill Latham and his wife were too wrapped up in the life of El Paso and First Baptist Church to leave when he retired as editor of the *El Paso Times*. "I met my wife on the steps of the church," Bill recalled. "We were married in the church. Most of our friends are still here. When the wedding ceremony was over, a couple of guys grabbed me and took me back into the hills. They were going to paint me with mercurochrome but I got away and walked back. Those fellows and are now on the deacon board. We've served together for more years than we like to remember.

"Our children are scattered now, but we decided not to follow them," Bill continued. "The biggest mistake you can make after retirement is to go and move in with your children who live in some distant place. We're happy staying in the same house and in the place where our roots are."

A house which comfortably held a whole family can become too big and expensive for a retired couple or single. "I moved in stages over several years," our pastor's mother-in-law, Mrs. William Owens, told me one morning at the parsonage, where she was visiting. "My husband died just before he was to retire. I moved from our big house in Atlanta to a smaller house, to an apartment, to a room in Wesley Woods, a Methodist facility for seniors. I love it there. I have lots of new friends. I can continue my outside activities and still attend the church which my husband and I helped organize twenty-seven years ago."

Most retirees live and die right in their old neighborhood. Still, thousands do move away. A wide range of retirement facilities are now available in most cities. These range from apartment houses and condo complexes to life-care facilities.

As to Bill Latham's warning about following your children, one risk is that those you follow will move again. The average American family moves about once every five years. If you have more than one adult child, which will you move near? Said a middle-aged Tennessean, "The eight of us live all over. We're happy that Mother and Dad decided to stay in the place we call home. We can all go visit there. And with relatives and friends all around, we don't worry about them being lonely."

Warm and sunny Florida and Arizona are hot spots for retirees. The warm ocean breezes are Florida's biggest attraction, although retirement vistas are now springing up in central Florida. The Orlando area, with Disney World, Epcot Center, and a host of beautiful lakes is a favorite of many. Miami has become much less desirable because of the frightening crime rate.

Arizona's lack of ocean beaches is more than compensated by the dry, invigorating desert climate, gem-like lakes, and magnificent mountains. It is less settled than Florida, although you wouldn't think that after being in Tucson and Phoenix. Like Florida, Arizona has come to have a high proportion of older citizens. You can walk for blocks and blocks in some localities of both cities and never see a child.

For the past three years, commuting from Chattanooga to Knoxville for my Ph.D., I've observed the migratory traffic to and from Florida. October and November are heavy months for travel south among snowbirds from Michigan, Ohio, and Ontario. By March and April they are coming back. Some are financially able to have two homes and enjoy the best of both worlds. Some are taking extended vacations to scout out the land before making the big move. Some have burned their bridges behind them and are taking all their worldly goods south. Traffic on other interstates headed toward retirement Meccas is just as heavy.

I've heard of whole neighborhoods of retirees moving from the North to Florida. Strictly speaking, this is not the case. But people from the same community, company, lodge, church, synagogue, or ethnic group do tend to migrate to certain areas. Boca Raton, for example, has become the retirement "place" for many northern evangelicals from Wheaton, Illinois, and Grand Rapids, Michigan. Back in 1950, Ira Eshelman started a Bible conference on the site of an old army barracks in Boca Raton: "Bibletown has since expanded to also include a large church which supports foreign missionaries, a Christian school, motel-like residence halls (named for famous evangelicals), and an apartment complex.

The typical story you hear in Boca Raton is: "We started coming for the Winter Bible Conference and then decided to move here."

Pat Zondervan, co-founder of the publisher that bears the Zondervan name, is chairman of Bibletown's board of trustees. Pat and his wife Mary started coming in 1956 when he was sixty. They now spend eight months of every year at their apartment in the complex. Still in vigorous health, Pat is only semi-retired. "We've been spending a little more time in Boca each year," he noted. "Last year we were here eight months." Pat continues as board chairman of the Zondervan Corporation and flies back for important meetings.

One day Marti and I joined Pat and Mary for lunch in a Boca restaurant. We had hardly sat down before Pat caught sight of a friend from Grand Rapids, then another from Wheaton. Throughout the meal, it was like old folks from home.

Boca Raton is not an evangelical ghetto. The population is a quarter million and growing. Nor is its income built on retirement communities. It is a microelectronic center for IBM, the biggest employer. It's a pleasant place to retire with balmy ocean breezes and a low crime rate. But housing is higher than in most Florida cities. Average selling price for a condominium is 1982 was $123,386; for a single family home, $155,027.

Wherever I talked to retirees about buying a new house, I heard the same counsel: Look around. Don't buy on first impressions. Watch the finances. Make certain the seller is legitimate, the title clear, the price right, and the neighborhood stable. Don't be fast-talked by a salesman.

Be sure this is the community where you want to live. Find a church in which you're comfortable before you buy. The pastor can be a good counselor. Check out cultural and recreational facilities attuned to your tastes.

Best of all, if you can manage, rent in the area or live in your trailer for awhile before buying.

Living in a life-care community is quite different from anywhere else. Residence is restricted to senior citizens, usually sixty and above. The other major distinction is that you are provided total or limited care for the rest of your life. For this you pay a founder's or entry fee upon admission, then a maintenance payment each month to cover services offered.

Marti and I visited Shell Point Village, one of the most attractive and best managed life-care facilities in the United States. Near Fort Myers, Florida, Shell Beach perches on a tropical peninsula, flanked by a bird life refuge on protected islands. Temperatures average seventy-four degrees Farenheit year round. The days are sunshiny, the water warm, the sunsets over the Gulf of Mexico breathtaking, and the lush gardens whisper paradise.

Shell Point Village is owned and operated by the Christian & Missionary Alliance, a small but respected evangelical Protestant denomination. When we were there, the entry fee for a single person in a semi-furnished studio apartment stood at $32,000 with a monthly maintenance charge of $439. For two persons in a two-bedroom apartment, the entry cost was $69,000 with $849 monthly for services. Meals in the dining hall were extra.

Shell Point's standard services for the monthly maintenance charge include all utilities except telephone, medical alert system in the apartment, physician on call twenty-four hours, nursing facility, laundry equipment, use of a recreational building and health club, social activities, woodworking shop, hobbies and craft programs, newspaper, library, guest house accommodations, swimming pool, boat docking, parking, eighteen-hole golf course, shuffleboard courts, post office, voting precinct, mini-market, beauty and barber shops, drug store, service station, inter-village transportation, bus service to shopping centers, village church, annual Bible conference, and concert season. In sum: total living with total care.

Shell Pointers range in age from sixty up. Some are in vigorous health and carry on full-time employment. At the other end of the spectrum, some are bed bound in the nursing facility. Residents can be as active as they wish and their energy permits. Many own their own cars and take extended trips. Residents are free to come and go as they would in other communities.

Villagers represent a wide cross-section of society. There are former carpenters, bricklayers, pastors, teachers, government workers, physicians, and executives. It is not necessary that one be a member of the sponsoring denomination or even a Christian, although most do attend the hexagonal-shaped church on the grounds. The church has a vigorous missionary outreach on every continent.

You can find both less expensive and more expensive communities than Shell Point Village. John

Knox Village in Lubbock, Texas, charges an entry fee from $18,950 to $44,950, depending on apartment size. Westminster-Canterbury House in Richmond, Virginia, runs from $33,265 to $88,210 with the monthly fee from $626 to $1,460. Fairhaven Community in Whitewater, Wisconsin, affiliated with the United Church of Christ, offers entry for as low as $12,000 with monthly maintenance of $242. However, the low Fairhaven cost excludes health care. If a resident is forced to move into an intermediate-care apartment, the monthly fee can go as high as $1,812.

A life-care home calls for a heavy investment. You may be making a lifetime commitment. So make a careful investigation before putting down any money and signing a contract.

What are the resources and reputation of the sponsor? Who will assume legal responsibility for corporation debts in case there are financial problems?

What does the actual contract cover? Don't depend upon a salesman's promise or rely on an advertising brochure. Find out what is standard service for the price offered and what is extra and optional.

Generally, there are two divisions of services. *Full care* includes almost everything, including all medical costs. Every resident pays a high monthly fee to insure this provision, although not everyone will need expensive health care. *Limited care* provides a limited amount of medical care. A certain number of days may be specified in the nursing unit, after which the monthly costs increase sharply.

What are the community's admission policies and rules? What rights do residents have? Is there a grievance committee to which residents can turn in a dispute with management?

Pay close attention to how transfer decisions are made. Who decides and by what criteria when a resident must be moved from an apartment to an intermediate-care unit, and from there to a nursing unit?

The American Association of Homes for the Aged has a directory listing about four hundred continuing-care homes. This is available for $10, plus $2.35, by writing to Publications, AAHA, 1050 Seventeenth St., N.W., Suite 770, Washington DC 20036.

Visit several full-care communities. Talk with residents. Stop by or call the local Better Business Bureau. Talk to a couple of area pastors. Then before signing, have your lawyer review the contract line by line.

One final word about life-care homes. The only depressing thing we noticed at Shell Point Village was the absence of children. We were told that children did come to visit, and to the village church, but we saw none on the Friday we were there. You can, of course, visit your grandchildren. You can see children on trips into town and vacations away. But children and young people, unless they are workers or guests, will be absent from community life.

Perhaps more critical than where you live is what you will be doing after retirement. Maybe you feel better than you did at fifty. You can't imagine yourself not working awhile longer, whether you need the income or not.

Opportunities will depend upon your pre-retirement employment, your skills, your initiative, and your willingness to scale down in time and money. If you're in good health, why worry about the diseases of old age? There's no law of nature that says you automatically begin a sharp decline after retirement. Between sixty-five and seventy-five there is very little change in health, according to Dr. James E. Birren, an authority on aging at the University of Southern California.

Take Daisy Grunau of Morriston, New Jersey.

Upon turning sixty-five, she had her bed moved downstairs in her home, expecting some dread illness to strike at any moment. Her health was good, but she had "just been programmed like everyone else to think sixty-five is the end of something." Bored and restless, she junked her second-class status, moved to El Paso, and took a job.

If you're self-employed, you can treat your sixty-fifth birthday like any other. You just have another year of good experience under your belt. Cameron Townsend led the Wycliffe Bible Translators into Colombia when he was sixty-five. At sixty-eight he opened a pavilion for Wycliffe at the New York World's Fair. At seventy-one he began studying Russian and the next year he made the first of eleven trips to survey Bibleless minority groups in the Soviet Union.

"Uncle Cam" was exactly twice my age when I accompanied him on a trip to Mexico City for interviews with government officials. At the end of two weeks I was mentally and physically exhausted from trying to keep up with this remarkable man. He died just this year, at eighty-five, not from old age but from acute leukemia.

OK, so you're not independent. Your employer has turned you out. Have you considered asking him if you can come back and work part time or serve as a consultant?

There's now a trend in this direction. Traveler's Insurance surveyed its employees fifty-five and over and found that 85 percent wanted some form of paid employment after retirement. In 1981 the company set up a labor pool of retired employees and filled more than half of all temporary jobs at the company with retirees.

Evelyn Smith is one of those brought back. She had been retired for a year, spending her time traveling, doing needlepoint, and attending club lunches. "That wasn't enough," she said. "I felt I needed to be on a schedule, for the structure and the stimulation."

Traveler's put her in charge of hiring the retirees.

Another is Robert Lawless, who retired in 1976 as assistant director of the data processing department. He now comes in on Tuesdays and Thursdays to help in expense management for Traveler's.

If you must look for remunerative work elsewhere, try first in the field in which you are known and/or have skills. A couple of days ago I talked to an old friend I hadn't seen in twenty years. I remembered that he was then an industrial sales manager. "What now?" I asked. "Oh, I turned sixty-five a couple of years ago and retired. I played golf and messed around the house for a few months. That wasn't enough. So I called on an old buddy and he put me to work a couple of days a week in his business."

So you can't think of an old buddy offhand. Start stirring your memory. Take a legal pad and make a column for each of your past twenty working years. Under each year jot down some of the projects in which you were involved and the names of work associates you remember. Don't attempt to complete this in an afternoon. Take a week or two and keep writing materials beside your bed. You may remember the name of a key person at one A.M. Whatever the result, I predict you'll be pleasantly surprised at the number of names you've dredged up.

Number them one, two, three, etc., in the order you think they can be helpful. Then get the addresses of the top twenty. If you know the metro areas where they live, look them up in telephone directories in the library. You may have to call old acquaintances for the addresses of some.

Personalize a letter to each one. Begin by recalling when you and he were last together. Briefly tell what has happened to you since, including your retirement. State some of your skills and responsibilities. Then ask the friend if he has any tips or leads for employment. Enclose a stamped addressed envelope and stick it in the mail.

Another idea is to purchase a "position wanted" ad in a trade magazine, a religious journal, or some other periodical which has readers from your field of work.

Don't be afraid to cross over, especially if your best skills are working with people. I have a friend who operates a tour service, providing customized travel for groups to the Holy Land, China, Europe, and many other faraway places. He has a number of tour reps who work on commission, enlisting friends and acquaintances to sign up for tours of their interest. Some reps organize their own tours and go along as the host. Some of these reps are retired ministers and professors. They're supplementing their pensions and having the time of their lives.

You may want to develop a small business. Doug Smith of Passaic, New Jersey, retired from an assembly line job and bought a van to transport older people to favorite eastern historical sites. He's making regular trips to places he loves and getting paid for it.

Whether working for yourself or someone else, follow this standard rule of success: Find a need and fill it. Then fit it into your other retirement plans.

Do you enjoy church work? You don't have to be a seminary-trained minister to get a job on a church staff. You might be a lay counselor, visit shut-ins, cook for special banquets, serve as part-time secretary for a full-time staff member, teach crafts, take charge of the library, or do some other task for remuneration. Most church jobs are voluntary, but some require employed personnel and are ideally suited for part-time people who are retired. If your church doesn't have anything, talk to the senior ministers of a few large churches around town.

A minister of a 5,000-member church told me recently: "We have eighteen people on our paid staff.

About half are over sixty-five. They're paid for part time, but some of them put in over forty hours a week. We couldn't get along without them."

If you don't need the money, you can just work for the simple joy of helping people. The opportunities are unlimited for volunteering.

Jim and Peggy Poor are two of the most exciting volunteers you'll ever meet. Remember them from chapter five? They married shortly before Jim's retirement and moved to Tucson. "I was going to do nothing but fish and play golf," Jim recalled. "But we joined a local church. That led to working with senior adults and that to attending a conference with representatives of other churches on ministries to retired folks."

"We just kept getting more and more involved," Peggy continued. "Helping other churches start senior adult programs, organizing retreats, serving on boards. Jim even served as president of the senior adult fellowship of our denomination in Arizona. And he had a big part in building several retirement homes across the state. Let him tell you about that."

"As we moved around, we saw this tremendous need for Christian retirement homes," Jim said. "We talked to church leaders and denominational officials. None wanted to get involved. So ten of us organized a non-profit corporation. We sold bonds, let contracts, hired management ourselves. Our first one in Phoenix already has ninety-nine residents and we're now making plans for one in another city."

Jim and Peggy showed me their calendar for the year. It was enough to boggle the mind: Senior Adult Banquet, Senior Adult Evangelism Conference, St. Patrick's Day Dinner, Senior Adult All Sports Day, USA Club Film, Senior Adult Sunday in Church, Adult Bible Conference, Senior Adult Craft Fair . . . on and on their schedule ran with something exciting for almost every week. Jim still golfs and fishes and also bowls (his high game is 279). And Peggy paints, teaches painting, plays the organ, swims, and maintains an exotic flower garden.

"We're having the time of our lives," Peggy declared. "We can't imagine what it is to be bored."

Floyd Pope, seventyish and a ramrod straight six-feet-two, is president this year of the sixty volunteers serving at Eastwood Hospital in El Paso. A retired seventh-grade science teacher, Floyd spends Tuesdays and Fridays there. "I do a lot of different things. Transport families of critically ill patients to the hospital. Pick up items from the pharmacy for medical personnel. Take patients around to different places for treatments. Make coffee in the family room for the families of patients in surgery. Mostly I listen and encourage. Often someone will thank me with tears in his eyes when all I've done is listen."

Floyd recalled one couple: "They sold their business up North and came to El Paso. They were down here without friends or family when the husband suffered a broken blood vessel near his heart. His wife couldn't accept the fact that he would probably die. It was a miracle he survived surgery. Then he had a relapse and recovered again. Throughout the ordeal, I had been talking to his wife. The third time he began sinking, she told me, 'I'm ready now.' He died a couple of days later."

Floyd also teaches seventh-graders in Sunday school at his church and takes church young people skating. "The kids keep me young. I skate right along with them." He's also been with the youth on trips to music festivals and church meetings in other cities. "My wife Lillian isn't physically able to go on these trips," he explained. "She stays home so I can go.

"When you retire, you must go on doing something and stay close to people," Floyd stressed. "I knew one man who was in great health when he retired. He didn't have a thing to do and was dead within a year. It helps to have something that doesn't stop when you're

LIFE CHANGES

sixty-five. I've been teaching seventh-graders in Sunday school for twenty-eight years. Some of my former students are married and now have children whom I'm teaching.

"You'd better stay in good physical shape, too, or you won't live to tell about it. I do about eleven different exercises for fifty minutes every day, except on Sunday. I've found this a good time to pray."

As to the value of volunteering, Floyd Pope pointed out: "You think you're helping others. And you are. But you're also helping yourself by getting your mind off your aches and pains."

Wrote Dr. Hans Selye, the renowned stress scientist: "Striving to make yourself ever more useful and necessary ... will protect you from the worst of all modern social stresses, purposelessness."

Don't overlook extended volunteer service with a religious or humanitarian agency, at home or abroad. This is not only an opportunity for early retirees but over-sixty-fivers as well.

I discovered hundreds of people serving extended terms of volunteer service, at home and overseas. Every organization I contacted said they were interested in retirees as volunteers. Some agencies will provide transportation and living accommodations for persons with special skills. Terms of service may range from two weeks to more than a year.

Service opportunities for volunteers are now routinely listed in many church periodicals. For example, an issue of *World Mission Journal* (Southern Baptist) notes under overseas needs:

> *Grenada*—Crafts teacher. One or two weeks. To teach prison inmates.
> *Costa Rica*—Two to three finish carpenters.

Needed for two to three weeks, cabinet and inside finish work.

Colombia—Elementary teacher for missionary children. Rent apartment or live with missionaries. Teach first and fourth grades to one child in each.

Nigeria—Maintenance engineer. Seminary. Three months.

Bophuthatswana—Veterinarian. One year. Transportation, housing provided.

Liberia—Librarian/secretary. One year assignment. Round-trip transportation and furnished housing provided.

This is only a partial listing for one month in one missionary periodical.

A volume could easily be filled with stories of volunteer retirees who have found fulfillment in serving through their church. Briefly, here are just a few:

Willard and Elsie Stokes retired from their Colorado grain farm and went to Ecuador with the Gospel Missionary Union. Willard intended to do maintenance work, but he soon saw the greater need for a film ministry. With a truck equipped to carry a portable generator, projector, and screens, the Strokeses traveled from village to village, showing Christian films to thousands of Quechua Indians. Then before coming home, Willard trained a national to operate the equipment and continue the ministry.

Art and Eleanor Taber came to the Wycliffe aviation center in North Carolina from a Chicago suburb. Art retired as a skilled mechanic for United Airlines. He went to work immediately on missionary planes being serviced for field work in South America, Africa, and Asia. Accustomed to the big jets, Art says, it "was hard to crawl around in the small planes. But I've learned to adjust." Eleanor, a retired school teacher, teaches kindergarten for missionary children and also has a Bible class at a local elementary school. "We love living here," Eleanor says. "For the first time in our lives we're both working full time for the same Employer."

Carl and Ethel Vinson lived in fifteen states while he worked forty years in exploration and research for the Exxon Oil Company. When Carl retired they moved to Magee, Mississippi, where they are teaching Laotian refugees to read and write in English. When word of the literacy program sponsored by a group of churches got around, the local sheriff invited Carl to teach literacy to prisoners. Carl and Ethel say they have received "much joy" through the "God-given ministries." They want to keep on "working for the Lord."

Joseph and Rose Birzler joined hands in making clothing for orphans sponsored by World Vision in Korea and Vietnam. Rose has sewn 8,800 dresses plus innumerable quilts, booties, shirts, pants, sweaters, and diapers. She once made twenty-seven dresses in one day. Yet Rose is legally blind in one eye and has only partial sight in the other. She also has a painful spinal ailment that makes it difficult to sit too long at her sewing machine. When she gets tired sewing, she joins Joe, a retired school custodian, in their garage where he stays busy packing and cutting out postcard-sized squares for Rose to make quilts.

Whatever your experience and interest, there is something important and life-fulfilling for you to do after sixty-five. You couldn't do better than take the motto of the National Retired Teachers Association: "To serve and not be served." And to heed advice from Arthur Clement, volunteer coordinator for the Citizen Representation Project (which trains older persons to serve in government agencies related to the needs of the elderly). Warned Mr. Clement: "If you don't remain active in some viable, meaningful interest you are going to deteriorate both bodily and mentally." Then, as a footnote, he observed: "My peers who remain alive are living longer."

So you're about to retire at sixty-five or seventy. For health and happiness' sake, don't settle down to a purposeless existence. Get involved in helping others.

8

Getting "Way Up There"

My Greatgrandpa Foster lived fifty miles from us—a "fur piece" in the Ozarks in the 1930s, if you had no car. But once a year the clan would gather for his birthday. There at the old home place where he had lived for sixty years, he would preside from his rocking chair over a grand dinner-on-the-grounds under spreading oak trees. We children would circle his chair, ogling his long white beard, which fell past the bib of his overalls, while he tried to guess which family we belonged to. He never knew who half of us were.

This patriarch of my mother's family died at ninety-five. I knew only one other person past ninety during my childhood, a gnarled, tart-tongued old hillbilly with an enormous walrus moustache that covered the tobacco stains around his mouth. When he came trudging down the dirt road, my cousins and I would chorus, "How're ye, Uncle Pete?" He would roll his dark eyes, aim a stream of tobacco juice, and snap back, "How'd ye like to be called, 'Hairy, Uncle Pete?'"

Uncle Pete, who wasn't really an uncle, and Greatgrandpa Foster probably stand out in my memory because so few lived past eighty and ninety in the 1930s. They were monuments to the ravages of time, ancients whom I thought must have been born before Washington.

Eightyish and ninetyish people are no longer oddities. A hundredth birthday does not merit an insert into Guinness. Not long ago I interviewed a frisky old preacher who claimed to be 110 years old. A Baptist evangelist, J. F. Akers said he was still preaching twenty revivals a year and had a missionary journey to Japan coming up. I went to the church where he was holding services one night. What a wonder! He bounded about on the platform for twenty minutes, quoting a whole chapter from the Old Testament, dramatizing the story of Elijah on Mount Carmel, and urging his listeners to "get on God's side." Then he sat down and preached for twenty minutes more. "I do this almost every night," he told me afterward.

His story sounded too good to be true. I called the newspaper in his hometown of Radford, Virginia, to verify his age. "Mr. Akers is an institution around here, but our research indicates he may not be as old as he claims to be," the editor said.

"How old do you think he really he?" I asked.

"Only 105. But we could be wrong. At his age, I suppose it doesn't make much difference."

Most of us living today will probably not reach the age of Preacher Akers. But half of all the babies born today can expect to live past seventy-five; over one fourth past eighty-five. If you're now in the sixty-five to seventy bracket, you can expect to reach eighty-two, if you're average.

"Old age" has been moved up a whole decade since World War II. When I was young a person was considered "old" at sixty. Many people now in their seventies and even eighties are in better condition than sixty-year-olds of a generation ago.

More of us are living longer and better, but only up to a point. Even if cardiovascular disease and cancer—still the deadliest killers—are conquered, physical life will only be nudged forward a few years.

Many researchers hold that every living creature is born with a biological "clock" that genetically ticks off the rate of aging. Our cells' immunity to disease steadily diminishes, vitality ebbs, organs deteriorate, and eventually death comes. The "clock's" location has not been found, but its existence has been pretty much determined by experiments, indicating that we are "appointed once to die," as the Bible says (Hebrews 9:27).

A few optimists believe that science will eventually learn how to repair or rewind the clock. They point to an experiment at the University of California at Irvine. Older mice, seventy years old in human terms, were given substances to repair damaged cell membranes. The rodents lived an average of 49 percent beyond their expected life spans. In other research, the age of test animals has been increased by altering the action of certain glands.

But most scientists maintain that living 200 years and beyond is only hopeful talk. Dr. Kurt Weiss, Professor of Physiology at the University of Oklahoma School for Health Sciences, told me bluntly, "We've gone about as far as we can go in extending the life span."

Still, if you're seventy or more, this is a great time to be alive. You need not sit and wither. The extent of what you can do for the rest of your life will likely be more limited by your attitude than your age. Seventy, eighty, ninety, or even one hundred is no reason to resign yourself to the "decrepit old age" of which William Butler Yeats lamented at sixty.

Your body may have more juice than you think. J. F. Akers, the spry preacher of whom I spoke a moment ago, enjoys pruning his fruit trees, although "my young wife doesn't like me to do it." His "young wife" is in her seventies.

My wife's maternal grandmother lived to her mid-nineties. When we lived in the Chicago area, her place in northern Michigan was within driving distance for a pleasant weekend. I recall arriving at Grandma Kleam's place late one snowy evening. At midnight she was waiting up for us with a pot of hot tea. "Shhh," she hushed our chattering daughters. "Mustn't wake up my old ladies upstairs." Grandma was then almost ninety. Her boarders were in their sixties and seventies.

Grandma Kleam took her first plane ride when she came to visit us at age ninety-three. We met her at O'Hare airport on a dark and stormy day. "Don't see why the weather had to be so bad for my first trip," she grumped. "Oh, you weren't in any danger from the bumps," I assured her. "Bumps!" she snorted back. "Who cares about bumps? I wanted to see something."

Not surprisingly, Grandma Kleam mowed her own lawn and put up her storm shutters until a short time before she died.

Four years ago, when I was only forty-eight, I took up running. I put in a lot of training miles, huffing and puffing to make a seven-and-a-half-minute mile, before entering my first race. How sweet it was to come in with the top 20 percent, ahead of many twenty- and twenty-five-year olds. How sweet—until I learned that two guys old enough for Medicare had averaged less than seven minutes a mile.

My goal is to run a marathon—twenty-six miles—without collapsing. If I make it next year, I'll still be far behind John A. Kelley, who recently marked his fifty-first Boston Marathon at age seventy-four.

Altogether, the indomitable John Kelley has run 109 marathons. He has won Boston twice, come in second seven times, and finished in the top ten, nineteen times. Last time he was far back of the top ten. Nevertheless, his loyal fans at the finish line were ready when they saw his white crown bobbing down the race course. "Here comes Kelley!" they screamed.

John Kelley's secret is to "keep in condition." He's up every morning at five and running by five-thirty. He logs about sixty-five training miles a week. No one-dimensional man, John also enjoys painting and tending two gardens during his retirement years.

"I just do the best I can day to day," he told a

reporter. "I wake up in the morning, shake my hand, and say, 'You made it.' All I want to do is finish the race in good shape." Some of his fans can imagine him running through the Pearly Gates to shouts of, "Here comes Kelley!"

Kelley has plenty of competition in athletics. Maude Hutton in Sun City, Arizona, hit a hole in one at eighty-four and is still stroking a mean golf game at ninety. Nellie Brown of Alexandria, Virginia, is eighty-seven and swims two thirds of a mile a day. She's the U.S. national champion in her age group. Nellie didn't start competitive swimming until eighty-one. Ninety-seven-year-old Luther Metkee of Camp Sherman, Oregon, keeps in shape by building log cabins. Luther had a sore finger when he was recently interviewed. "Can't think about that," he declared. "Got some logs to hew." Philosophizes Luther: "When you stop having anything to think about but yourself, it isn't long before all you want to do is think about yourself."

There's plenty more to warm your bones. Florence London, a resident of the Big Apple, swims like a fish at eighty-three and plays a tough game of tennis. "I don't like the word 'retire,'" she declares. "I use that word when I go to bed to sleep."

Fred Knoler, just eighty-five, zips around Fort Lauderdale, Florida, on a bike. Except when he's pedaling in bike races somewhere else. Fred's fastest time to date is eighty-nine minutes in a twenty-mile race. He hopes to do better.

And you've got to look up to George E. Bowman. Seventy-one and a retired welder, George makes three or four parachute jumps a month. He intends to keep on jumping until at least age eighty. Parachuting, he says, "grows on you. It's something you don't want to give up, once you've experienced it. No matter how old you are."

Think you're too old? Get out of that rocking

chair and look around at the number of folks who refuse to conform to society's stereotypes. You'll be surprised at the number who are still daring and doing and making faces at Father Time. Catch their spirit. Get in the swim of life with them. Don't be like the retired plumber of whom his wife said, "All the exercise he gets is letting his flesh creep while he lies on the couch reading Agatha Christie."

Physical conditioning will make your years both longer and richer. You don't have to run marathons. Vigorous walking, says Dr. Fred A. Stutman, is sufficient for most people.

Dr. Stutman concedes that heredity is a big factor in how long you live. But the less active you are, he emphasizes, the faster the aging process increases, making you more vulnerable to psychological and physical problems. The more active you are, particularly in aerobic exercises such as walking, running, bicycling, and swimming, the slower you will age. Aerobics expands your capacity for energy and endurance, while combating heart and circulatory disease.

Of course you have limitations. Everybody has, even twenty-year-olds. You just become more aware of what you can't do as you get older. But this awareness may come less from reality and more from what you've been taught are the limitations of old age. The following poem by an anonymous author, who is probably long dead, illustrates what I mean:

How do I know my youth is all spent?
My "get up and go" has got up and went.
My joints are now stiff and filled with pain.
The pills that I take, they give me no gain.
I rub in the ointment, the best I can do.
Each pain when it leaves, comes back with two.
But in spite of it all, I am able to grin,
When I think of the places my "get-up" has been.

> *Old Age is Golden, I have heard it said,*
> *But sometimes I wonder, as I get into bed.*
> *My "ears" on the dresser, my "teeth" in a cup.*
> *My "eyes" on the table, until I get up.*
> *Ere sleep comes each night, I say to myself,*
> *Is there anything else I should lay on the shelf?*
> *Yet, I am happy to know as I close the door,*
> *My friends are the same, as the days of yore.*
> *When I was young, and my slippers were red,*
> *I could kick up my heels, high over my head.*
> *When I grew older, my slippers were blue,*
> *I could still dance, the whole night through.*
> *But now I am old, and my slippers are black.*
> *I creep to the store, and puff my way back.*
> *Yet, I really don't mind, I say with a grin,*
> *When I think of the places, my "get-up" has been.*
> *Since I have retired from life's competition,*
> *Each day is filled with complete repetition.*
> *I'm up in the morning, and dust off my wits,*
> *Go pick up the paper and read the "obits."*
> *If my name isn't there, I know I'm not dead.*
> *I get a good breakfast, and go back to bed.*
> *The reason I KNOW, my youth is all spent,*
> *My "get up and go" has got up and went.*

The poem is funny, but a bit depressing. The writer is living as if his whole life is over. He thinks he can only go back and relive his lost youth. For the rest of his life he sees only repetition.

Reminiscing may be nice for an occasional rainy day. A day when you can't find anything more exciting to do. But beware of boring your friends. Unless you're a born story teller, your supply of listeners could get up and go.

If you're caught in the reminiscing swamp; if reliving the past has kept you from speaking of the present and future; if you find yourself getting up in the morning with nothing to do but remember the "good old days"; if you're constantly looking back instead of ahead—then better shift gears now and take your life out of reverse.

Of course it's OK, and healthy, to reflect on the past now and then. Especially on the goodness of God. Frequently in the Old Testament, the Hebrews were exhorted to remember what God had done for them. As King David urged when the ark of the covenant was brought up to Jerusalem: "Remember his marvellous works that he hath done, his wonders, and the judgments of his mouth" (1 Chronicles 16:12). What you must not do is dwell on past failures. Nor think you have accomplished all that God intended. Say with Paul: "I do not regard myself as having laid hold of it yet; but one thing I do: forgetting what lies behind and reaching forward to what lies ahead, I press on toward the goal for the prize of the upward call of God in Christ Jesus" (Philippians 3:13, 14, NASB).

Eyes ahead. Forward march. Is there a river before you? Wade in. The cold current will galvanize your bones. A mountain beyond the far bank? Move on. Move up ... up ... up. Think of the boulders as opportunities to climb on. Ignore the quitters calling from below that it can't be done. Be like the little train that chugged up its mountain, announcing with every puff, "I think I can! I think I can!" Then as it neared the top: "I know I can! I know I can!" Visualize yourself setting foot on the summit. Feeling the cool wind from the other side. Seeing the vistas of the Shangri-la before you. YOU CAN DO IT!

Take a cue from "Miz" Patsy Turner, long a legendary missionary figure in the hills of eastern Kentucky. Miz Patsy started schools, planted churches, tamed moonshiners, and spread the gospel for decades among her beloved mountain people. She passed her sixty-fifth birthday and made no move to retire. Sixty-sixth and nothing said. Sixty-seventh. An official reminder came from the headquarters of the Presbyterian Church in the U.S., her sponsor, that she was past the age when missionaries were supposed to quit, or at least slow down. Miz Patsy kept thundering ahead.

After she had ignored several requests to retire, an official committee came calling. They sat on Miz Patsy's porch and talked. "Miz Patsy," the chairman said softly, "you've done more than your part. It's time to rest on your accomplishments. Why don't you find yourself a good home and enjoy your old age?"

Miz Patsy looked across her green valley. She saw smoke spiralling from the cabin chimneys of her friends. She thought of the children from those homes who would never have gotten an education if she had not come to the mountains. She thought of others who needed her help.

The longer the chairman talked, the more the fire built in her eyes. Finally she could stand it no longer. "I reckon I'm not ready yet," she declared with the set of her chin. "I reckon that as long as I'm alive, I intend to live. That means staying here, whether the church supports me or not."

Season turned upon season. The members of the church committee who had called on her, retired. On her hundredth birthday, headquarters asked her to come to Richmond, Virginia, for special honors. After the speeches were made and the applause died, someone asked if now she intended to take a rest. "Why should I?" she responded. "What else would I do besides be a missionary? I reckon I'll just keep on."

Miz Patsy returned to the mountains and lived to be 105.

So society says you should quit. So your family is pressuring you to take it easy and "enjoy" the rest of your life. So what. Tell them you'll not put down the reins until you see the undertaker coming, and not a minute before.

Be like Miz Patsy Turner: As long as you're alive, intend to LIVE.

Never mind those who have given up and surrendered to the whim of relatives. Take heart from the "Miz Patsys" who are defying tradition, society, and the caution of well-meaning relatives. It bears repeating that you're likely to live longer if you have a purpose to stay alive, and if you're busy fulfilling that purpose.

There's Herbert Lockyer, Sr., a bare ninety-five, who has just finished compiling his 300,000 word *Lockyer Dictionary of the Bible*. Having already written over sixty books, he calls his *Dictionary*, "the most colossal task of my life." He started on it when he was past ninety.

Dr. Lockyer, who has his own apartment in Colorado Springs, works six or seven hours every day except Sunday. He also keeps an exhaustive schedule of speaking engagements.

And he writes every word by longhand. A typewriter is "too cold" for him.

Across the Atlantic, Dr. Lockyer's friend, Dr. T. Wilkinson Riddle, is editor-in-chief of the *Christian Herald* of England. Four months senior to Dr. Lockyer, Dr. Riddle is the world's oldest active editor, according to the *Guinness' Book of Records*. After three trips to surgery, he had difficulty moving about, but he still manages to write and edit. Dr. Riddle, like Dr. Lockyer, is a widower. "In some ways, I am like Elijah who said, 'I alone am left,' " he says. "Yet I'm not alone, for his rod and staff are my abiding comfort and support."

Major Harvey Banks of the Salvation Army was a bit older than Drs. Riddle and Lockyer when he passed away recently in Atlanta—at 109 to be exact. He was the oldest "retired" Salvation Army officer in the world.

He retired back in his sixties, when his health took a downward turn. But he couldn't stay idle and was soon back visiting jails and prisons, singing and playing music, and sharing his faith with prisoners. When a flood or some other disaster came along, he was always there helping the survivors, even when he was over one hundred. An old friend noted, "He lived on faith. He used the extra energy God gave him in the interest of other people."

The unstoppable "Mother" George didn't get to Africa as a missionary until she was thirty-five. Black missionaries from the U.S. were exceedingly rare seventy years ago and it was difficult to find a church agency that would support one. She performed a heroic ministry of starting schools and churches in the Liberian bush for the next thirty-five years. Then, in 1945, her sponsor, the National Baptist Convention, retired her at seventy.

She raised her own support and went back. At seventy-two she planted a mission station in a "cursed place" where no decent Liberian would dare live. By age 100 she had started over a hundred churches, a training school, two high schools, and a technical school.

When she came home for her hundredth birthday, admirers gave a parade in her hometown of Greenville, Texas. A big banner said it all:

HER LIFE WAS THE BEST COMMENTARY
OF THE BIBLE
WE HAVE EVER READ
MOTHER ELIZA DAVIS GEORGE
THE GREAT GENERAL
OF THE MISSIONARY ARMY OF THE LORD.

Over thirteen-thousand centenarians are living in the U.S. right now, and the number is growing every day. The oldest was once thought to be Florida's Charlie Smith, who steadfastly insisted that he was born in 1842.

However, a marriage license has been found on which he gave his age at thirty-five in 1910. If this is correct, he lived to be only 104 (he died in 1979).

Arthur Reed of Oakland, California, may now be America's oldest living senior. Social Security records indicate that he was born in 1860, the year Abraham Lincoln was elected president.

Arthur worked for Phoenix Ironworks in Oakland until he was 116. He jokes about "not having had a job since." He claims to be looking for a new wife, preferably one between eighteen and thirty-five.

The oldest people in the world are reported to live in three widely separated rural mountainous areas, the Andes of Ecuador, the Caucasuses of the Soviet Union, and the hills of northern Pakistan. Dr. David Davies, a London gerontologist, found an Ecuadorian man and wife, aged 145 and 140 respectively. Another Ecuadorian was said to have died at 168. Dr. Davies claims baptismal certificates prove scores of oldsters in the Andes to have lived past 110.

Similar claims are made for people in the other two regions. The late Dr. Cameron Townsend and his wife Elaine visited the Caucasuses and were introduced to several couples said to be observing their one hundredth wedding anniversaries. However, documentation is lacking.

The oldest people on record lived before the great flood of Noah. According to Genesis, Adam lived to be 930 and his son Seth attained the age of 815. Methuselah, oldest of the biblical antediluvians, reached 969. Noah died at the age of 950. Think what a nine-century lifespan would cover in more recent times. If Noah lived today he would have been born in the eleventh century A.D. His lifetime would have included the Renaissance, Reformation, birth of America, industrial revolution, two world wars, the development of electricity, the telephone, the automobile, the airplane, nuclear energy, space flight, and the computer chip. What a lot he would have to tell his grandchildren.

Did people really live to be that old before the flood? Could time have been computed differently? A time difference could only have occurred if planet earth had then been revolving around the sun in much less than a present year. Genesis 1:14 suggests that earth's movement was pretty well fixed from the beginning.

The most reasonable explanation is that disease, a result of man's fall from Edenic innocence, was just beginning to corrupt the earth. The environment was still relatively pure. The gene chain which passes on life-shortening proclivities, possibly including an aging clock, was just starting to become contaminated.

These conditions kept worsening as a result of the Fall and man's continued disobedience. After the flood, life expectancy became progressively shorter. By the time of Moses, a lifespan of seventy was considered normal, although Moses himself was still vigorous at 120. The anticipated threescore and ten probably did not take into consideration childhood deaths from diseases, epidemics, and war. Average life expectancy may have been no more than thirty.

Length of life has not been greatly increased beyond threescore and ten in over three millenniums since. What medical science has done is to help more people live as long as a few did many years ago.

Not surprisingly to those who believe the Scriptures to be divinely inspired, the science of gerontology has come to support the Bible in describing the ingredients for longevity.

Biblical old age signified lifelong fear of the Lord and keeping of his commands (Leviticus 19:32; Deuteronomy 30:19, 20). "The hoary head is a crown of glory, if it be found in the way of righteousness" (Proverbs 16:31). "He that will love life, and see good days, let him refrain his tongue from evil, and his lips that they speak no guile" (1 Peter 3:10). The Bible also speaks of God's judgment for idolatry in "visiting the iniquity of the fathers upon the children unto the third and fourth generation" (Exodus 20:5). Idolatry was much more than merely bowing down to an idol. It called for adopting the perverted life style of the pagan religion, which was often marked by sexual promiscuity and the spread of sexually transmitted diseases.

Gerontologist Stephen Jewett's classic study of long-lived persons in New England produced this profile of longevity. Note how the characteristics coincide with biblical principles.

Good heredity. Parents and the grandparents of the very old tended to live a long time. (Scripture teaches that both obedience and disobedience to God's laws have effects upon future generations.)

Good marital and sexual relationships. The long-lived were more apt to be married and have strong sex drives. (Far from being anti-sex, the Bible calls for sexual commitment and submission on the part of both husbands and wives.)

Good physical health. The elderly whom Jewett studied had maintained good health and kept their weight within reasonable bounds. (The Bible calls for temperate living and warns against defilement of the body which is the temple of the Holy Spirit.)

Good work habits. The New Englanders tended to be independent and self-sufficient workers. (The much-maligned Protestant work ethic is straight out of the Bible. Enjoinders to work extend from Genesis to the epistles. "The Lord God ... put him [Adam] into the garden of Eden to dress it and to keep it" (Genesis 2:15). "We command ... that with quietness they work, and eat their own bread" (2 Thessalonians 3:12).

Reduced anxiety. Dr. Jewett's subjects were not worriers. Scripture assures believers that they need not worry. For example: 1 Peter 5:7: "Casting all your care upon him; for he careth for you." And John 14:27: "Peace I leave with you; My peace I give to you; not as the world gives, do I give to you. Let not your heart be troubled, nor let it be fearful" (NASB).

Optimistic. Dr. Jewett's people tended to have kept a sunny outlook on life. Scripture brims with reasons for optimism, confidence, and a sense of security for believers. Consider just two verses. Romans 8:28: "We know that God causes all things to work together for good to those who love God, to those who are called according to His purpose" (NASB). And 2 Timothy 1:12: "I know whom I have believed and I am convinced that He is able to guard what I have entrusted to Him until that day" (NASB).

Realistic. The long-lived New Englanders tended to live in the present and not dwell on the past. "Now" is a much-used biblical word. "The life I *now* live" (Galatians 2:20). "The life that *now* is" (1 Timothy 4:8). "*Now* we are sons of God" (1 John 3:2).

Moderate eating. Dr. Jewett's subjects tended to eat regularly but not in excess. Overeating is a biblical sin. "Put a knife to thy throat, if thou be a man given to appetite" (Proverbs 23:2). In this same chapter, verse 21, the glutton is listed with the drunkard.

Religious. All of Dr. Jewett's subjects considered themselves religious. Many said they were devout. "Fear [reverence] of the Lord prolongeth days: but the years of the wicked shall be shortened" (Proverbs 10:27).

Jewett's study was made quite a number of years ago. Research since then tends to keep confirming his findings. This is to be expected since the principles of living a good and long life are embedded in Scripture and "the word of the Lord endureth for ever" (1 Peter 1:25).

Those who live by God's principles and rules become caught up in a positive cycle where good habits interact and provide mutual reinforcement. Conversely, those who flout God's commands become trapped in a negative cycle in which bad practices develop into a destructive pattern of interaction and mutual corruption. "Be not deceived; God is not mocked: for whatsoever a man soweth that shall he also reap" (Galatians 6:7).

For sure, you can find exceptions, such as Pablo Picasso, who lived to ninety-two, and Bertrand Russell, who reached ninety-eight. Both flouted biblical morality and lived a long time. Both were brilliant but troubled in their old age. How much happier lives both might have had, had they walked in God's ways. And each might have lived ten years longer.

A ninety-year-old who swears, is irreligious, and indulges every appetite makes news because he is unusual. The great majority of those who live a long time are temperate and God-fearing.

Perhaps you heard of the gerontologist doing research in a public park. He came upon a man, stooped and bent, wrinkled and gray, shuffling along a leaf-strewn path. "Say, old timer," the investigator said, "would you tell me the secrets of your age?"

The pitiable figure rasped in a tired voice. "I get drunk twice a week, chase every woman I can, and eat like a hog."

"And how old are you?" the scientist asked.

"Best I recollect, I was thirty-three on my last birthday. Now can I run along? A friend is waiting for me with a jug of wine."

I was contemplating the *real* secrets of longevity when my alumni newspaper arrived from Ouachita Baptist University. A headline proclaimed:

OUACHITA GRAD EARNS PH.D. AT 92

I had never heard of Virgil Conner. Probably because he graduated in 1912, thirty-eight years before my class. The report said he had worked in real estate and insurance until eighty, then turned over the business to "young Virgil," his sixty-four-year-old son. In 1970, at eighty-two, he enrolled in graduate school at Florida State University. Studying part time, he attained his doctorate ten years later—the oldest person known to have received a Ph.D. "Dr." Virgil Conner was still working, serving as a dollar-a-year research aide to a Florida legislator.

Later I saw a newspaper story on "Old Virgil's" achievement. "Why is what I've done being called a phenomenon?" he was quoted as asking. "To me, this is the most normal type of development for a human being."

One afternoon while pursuing my own graduate studies at the University of Tennessee, I saw the clipping about Virgil Conner in the carrel of a student I knew. Alice Gagnard at twenty-three happened then to be the youngest student in UT's College of Communications. "He's an alumnus from the school I attended," I told Alice proudly.

"Really," she replied. "He's an inspiration to me." A year later Alice received her Ph.D., becoming the first ever to attain a perfect four point average in doctoral studies in the college.

I ran into the remarkable Mary Bowman at First Baptist Church, El Paso, where she is the oldest member of the ministry staff. At eighty-seven, Mary had a long list of shut-ins and hospital patients to visit that day. "My job is to cheer them up and let them know that God cares," she said.

I asked about her health. "Had a little spell with my heart five years ago and got a triple bypass. My doctor told me then I might be getting a little too old to keep working. I said, 'Listen, Joe, I've got the green light from Above. Just get this surgery over with and let me get back to helping folks.'"

Mary was born in Hungary, emigrated to Texas

LIFE CHANGES

by way of Mexico, and was left a widow with four young children to support during the Great Depression. She has been a salaried church worker since sixty-two, an age when many people are thinking of quitting work. "I drive my own car to the church. The secretary gives me a list of folks that need visiting and I hit the road. People I visit often say, 'You've made my day by coming,' I tell them, 'If I can make your day, then you've made my day.'"

Mary reminds me of Lowell Thomas, whom I never knew except as a fan of his news broadcasts. Young Lowell was raised on the Bible. His earliest speech training came in declaiming Bible verses from the pulpit of his family's church while his father listened from the last pew. For almost seventy years, Lowell traveled the world, broadcasting from wherever he happened to be. He may have attained more firsts than "any man since Adam." He was the first to broadcast from a coal mine, a mountaintop, an airplane, a ship, a helicopter, and a submarine, not to mention his daring feats as an explorer. When he was eighty-three, his wife of fifty-eight years died. He remarried two years later and flew off to Tibet, ignoring a minor heart problem. He continued making regular broadcasts almost to his death at eighty-seven. Lowell Thomas' cheery, "So long until tomorrow," still echoes in my ears.

The other night I was coming home on a flight from Atlanta and happened to sit next to a gentleman who looked sixty or so. "No, I'm eighty," Dr. Gordon Clark said proudly. When he gave his name, I recognized a world-renowned Christian philosopher and author of over twenty-five books. "Still writing?" I asked. "Certainly, and teaching systematic theology at Covenant College on Lookout Mountain. That makes us neighbors," he noted.

Another "neighbor" is Dr. Karl Hujer, professor emeritus of astronomy and physics and director emeritus of the Jones Observatory at the University of Tennessee at Chattanooga. Dr. Hujer just turned eighty. Last I heard he was heading for Mexico to study Mayan and Aztec astronomy, then to Peru for research on Inca star-gazers, then to China and India to study astronomy in the Sanskrit language.

Mrs. B. B. McKinney is just up the Interstate a piece—living in Nashville. her late husband is the most famous hymn writer in my denomination. At ninety-two, Mrs. McKinney is far from being ready for a rest home. She keeps up with her departed husband's business affairs, answering up to 150 letters a month. She also travels and speaks across the country—all despite a serious hearing impairment. "The way to live a long time," she says, "is to avoid head colds, get plenty of rest, eat well-balanced meals, and keep active."

Roy Acuff seems to go on forever. As a boy in the Ozarks, I heard him every Saturday night over an old battery radio. I was up at the Grand Ole Opry a few months ago and there was Roy doing "The Wabash Cannon Ball," his voice almost as mellow as it was thirty-five years ago. The other night I saw him with the "Hee-Haw" gang, fiddling and laughing and telling jokes. Hard to believe from looking at him that Roy Acuff, the "King of Country Music" is almost eighty years old. Roy's wife died last year and he's had a few health problems himself. But he's still entertaining and making people smile. He recently moved from his big house to an apartment back of the Roy Acuff Museum, just a short walk from the gate of the Nashville theme park, "Opryland U.S.A." If Roy doesn't die with a fiddle in his hand, he'll go while signing autographs at his museum.

I get a kick out of crusty Frank Wheaton, who just passed the century mark and continues as chairman of the board of Wheaton Industries in Milville, New Jersey. "Retirement," Frank says, "is a sure shortcut to the grave. It used to be people would retire at seventy, then it got to be sixty-five. Nowadays they want to quit at sixty or sixty-two. And for what? To sit and wish they had something to do."

"Keeping busy" is the secret of Frank's long life. "For most of this century my employees have been coming to tell me they are going to retire. Every time they do I warn them that even at my age I will outlive them. So far, I have."

There are many more.

Appy Kroll, a spry 107 in Spokane, Washington, takes care of her eighty-year-old son, Bill.

Dr. Elizabeth Crosby is ninety-four and gets about on crutches while teaching neurology at the University of Michigan.

Dr. Howard Nash, ninety-six, still practices medicine in a tiny office in Atlanta. "God put me in charge of this spot," he declares. "It's up to me to take care of it."

Dr. Charles H. Wesley, ninety, is writing two books. He rides a bike and does 100 pull-ups daily for exercise. He'd rather "drop than just sit down."

And there's Harry Lieberman of Long Island, New York, who admits to 105. Harry is probably the world's oldest working artist. Back in 1950 Harry retired from a successful candy company, and soon found himself bored. "I didn't know when to wake up and when to go to sleep." He took up chess and a few other pursuits, then turned to painting in his late seventies, about the same age as Grandma Moses, who lived to be 101. During the past twenty-four years Harry has painted over a thousand pictures. "When I was younger I would paint sixteen hours a day. Now that I'm older, I don't sit in a chair for more than two hours a day. Old age has its limitations."

Indeed it does, as any person past seventy knows. Your arteries aren't as clear as they once were.

Your legs aren't as mobile. Your eyes and ears are less sharp. But then everybody has some limitations. At seventy and beyond you're just a little more limited.

But as George Burns says, "You can't help getting older, but you don't have to get old." You are old when you think you have nothing more to do but vegetate until your heart stops beating and your lungs quit breathing. You are old when you see nothing else to do but wait for the end.

To keep from getting old you'll have to fight stiff headwinds of social stereotypes, family expectancies, and your own aches and pains. If you do nothing, you'll be forced backwards to the rocking chair, the mattress, and eventually to the grave. To keep from getting old, you have to fight. To cite a sports cliche: When the going gets tough, the tough get going. Now when it is tougher than ever, you must get going and keep going, even while the going is greatly restricted.

So you've got a physical problem. Perhaps a little more than a problem. Crippling arthritis? Fast fading sight? Zooming blood pressure? A worn-out ticker? Impaired hearing that picks up only a shout? Inoperable cancer?

Every day, hour, and minute you must keep believing there is something for you to do with the rest of your life. Along with believing, you must keep looking, and when you find something to do, then do it. Remember, you aren't dead until you are dead. And then, if you are a believer, your real life will just be beginning as you become fully alive to God.

Nelly May Rowe is eighty-three and weakened by cancer. Yet this brave Black woman who once lived in a two-room Georgia shack keeps drawing and sewing and making her famous gum-chewing sculptures. Her art is seen in museums around the world. It was displayed at the Knoxville World's Fair.

Nelly is sure that one day, soon, the Lord "will give me my little wings. I'm ready to fly to heaven on them. But I don't think he's ready for me to start flappin' em yet." So she keeps on working. Work makes the pain more bearable.

Welthy Fisher, age 103, is the world's first lady of literacy. A former missionary, she's a legend in India where she is credited with helping multitudes to read and write. Friends say she was always in a hurry. She tells people that to live to be 100, you "get to be ninety-nine, and then you're very careful." Her friends laugh because she has never seemed overly careful. Once in her nineties she broke a bone on her way to a conference and had to lie on the hall floor until the doctor came. Seeing her friends' worried faces, she said, "Well, what are we waiting for? Pull up your chairs around me, and we'll go ahead with the conference."

Now blind in one eye, Welthy also suffers from painful arthritis. Yet according to a close companion, her attitude is, "Why stop now?"

Clara Elliot is the mother of Jim Elliot, one of the five heroic missionaries killed by savage Auca Indians in 1956. Clara's husband died in 1970, at the age of eighty-three. Arthritis later forced Clara to give up her chiropractic practice. She turned to a correspondence and prayer ministry with missionaries. Her hands are now so crippled she can barely write a letter, but she keeps trying. She also continues to do her own housework and cooking.

Welthy Fisher, Nelly May Rowe, and Clara Elliot have the same spirit as my neighbor's eighty-six-year-old father. "Dad's blind in one eye," Dean Styers says. "His legs were recently amputated. He has all kinds of reasons not to do anything, yet he never complains. When I asked him his secret, he said, 'Son, I look forward to what I can see in the morning, not what I can't see.' "

Unless death should suddenly intervene, there

will likely come a time when you can no longer care for yourself. After my Grandpa Foster lost his hearing, Grandma Foster became almost blind. She became his ears and he her eyes. As the eldest of their six children, my mother felt responsible for their welfare. When Grandpa could no longer tend a garden or feed and milk their cow, Mother moved them to a small house just down the hill from where she and Daddy lived. Unable to stand alone or sit in a chair, Grandpa was taken to bed. One evening Mother called me in Illinois to say Grandpa was near death. A day's drive brought me to his bedside. I shouted into his ears and he opened his eyes and recognized me. We talked about our last fishing trip together. "Boy, we really caught a string, didn't we?" I yelled. Grandpa smiled back. Then he closed his eyes and slept. Two weeks later he was dead.

Grandma stayed on alone in her little house. She could get to Mother and Dad's house with the aid of her cane, but she had to be led the quarter mile to the church near the brow of the hill. One day a dog knocked her off balance. She broke her hip in the fall. Complications kept her in the hospital. Once again a call came: "Grandma is going. Come at once."

Thin and frail, she looked like an oversized doll under the white sheet. I had been told she was in a coma and could not speak. Still I whispered, "Grandma, it's James." There was no answer. "Grandma, Jesus loves you. Do you know that?" Perhaps it was my imagination, but I was sure a trace of a smile showed on her face. Then, to the surprise of everyone gathered around, she began reciting lines from an old hymn. I bent close to catch all the words:

> *A guilty sinner once was I*
> *Thy righteous law condemned to die.*
> *One hope remains; one only plea:*
> *Jesus the Savior died for me.*

He died to save the world from sin.
He died from death my soul to win.
With Him my hope shall ever be;
He died for me; He died for me.

Her lips fell silent. She talked no more that day. Shortly after I returned home she slipped away to her eternal home.

An overwhelming sense of hopelessness may come when you think there is no recovery from a present ailment. Perhaps you have been told to set your house in order. Or you've lost your spouse or suffered some other great sorrow. A dark night settles in. You don't care to eat or bathe. You have nothing to say when someone comes to visit. Everything looks black. You think slower, act slower, worry endlessly over decisions, and have trouble concentrating.

There may be some small comfort in knowing you are not alone. Depression affects more of the elderly than any other age group. It is also the number one cause of suicide among people your age. Yet depression need not be the end.

Whatever you do, don't give up. Don't accept the snap diagnosis of an ill-informed friend or relative. For starters, I recommend you read the chapter on depression from Dr. James D. Mallory's *Untwisted Living* (published in paperback by Victor Books; available at your Christian bookstore). Dr. Mallory, whom I quoted earlier, is a Christian. He has worked with elderly depressed people. He understands your problems. He has excellent advice on how to deal with depression.

He says the causes of depression are many, and they frequently interact to make the condition worse. Depression may be inherited, making some persons more depression prone than others. Temperament may play a part. Environment and circumstances may be involved. Alcohol, certain medicines, and other chemical substances may be among the causal forces. Spiritual factors such as guilt may be in the picture.

The good news, according to Dr. Mallory, is that about 85 percent of depression victims can be successfully treated. The best treatment is a total program for relief. Medication, counseling, praying, confessing, and repenting may all be necessary. Seek help from all resources available, including physicians who know what medication to prescribe. Dr. Mallory cautions that not all physicians are prepared to deal with depression. If you aren't satisfied with your doctor's help, ask him for a referral.

Don't give up. Don't let your condition be written off as senility when your problem may be depression. Many forms of senility are not hopeless. Only a small percentage of the population has the dread Alzheimer's Disease, and researchers are searching for a way to arrest this affliction.

Still there will come a time when you will face your last illness. Short of the return of our Lord Jesus Christ, we will all come to the final scene of life. The curtain will ring down sooner for some of us than others. But it will descend.

I suggest that you tell your loved ones and doctor now how you wish to be treated during your last illness. My wife and I were discussing this the other night. "When I'm ready to die," she said, "please don't let them keep me alive as a vegetable. Let me go." You may feel the same way, but your loved ones need to know that.

Dr. Christopher M. Reilly, a past president of the Christian Medical Society, says an ethical physician has only two options in treating the terminally ill patient:

    1. Active treatment for maximum lengthening of life.

2. Passive management to shorten the dying process.

Your physician must weigh these options against a variety of other factors, including: the level of pain (often the doctor cannot relieve pain without shortening life), the financial impact of further expensive treatment on your family, and the use of medical care and equipment which may be needed by another patient with better chances for surviving.

Your doctor will not want to "play God." He will only want to follow the wishes of you and your family. It is best that you tell them now, especially if you are harboring a terminal disease. Later you may not be able to make the choice. You may do this orally; however, a written statement is more likely to be followed.

You need not fear death if you are a Christian and live in the presence of the Savior, who has triumphed over death. For you, Christ has died and risen. Death has lost its sting and the grave its victory (1 Corinthians 15:55). You know that this life is not all there is, and that to depart and be with Christ is far better. Indeed, as a believer, you are already experiencing "eternal life," a quality of life that continues. Death is not the end, but only a transition from one stage of eternal life to another. Then you will no longer "see through a glass, darkly; but . . . face to face" (1 Corinthians 13:12). When you see death approaching, you can say as the beautiful Ann Judson did to her suffering missionary husband: "Oh, the happy day will soon come when we shall meet all our friends who are now scattered—meet to part no more in our Heavenly Father's house."

Now that you are older, heaven should be much more meaningful to you. When I was twenty or thirty, I did not think much of heaven. I now have a deeper longing to see departed friends and loved ones. What a joy it will be to greet them. Should the Lord spare me until eighty, the reunion will be all the more wonderful, for there will be many more to see.

Whatever your situation, the most important question is not, "What are you going to do with the rest of *this* life?" but, "What are you going to do with the living Lord?"

He came that you might have life and have it more abundantly (John 10:10). He invites, "Come unto me, all ye that labour and are heavy laden, and I will give you rest" (Matthew 11:28). He promises, "Behold, I stand at the door, and knock: if any man hear my voice, and open the door, I will come in to him, and will sup with him, and he with me" (Revelation 3:20).

The most important question, the ultimate question for this life and that which is to come is: "What are you going to do with Jesus the Messiah and Savior?"

Settle this question first, then tackle the lesser ones that come with life's changes and transitions. Whether you're bogged down in midlife, unemployed, widowed, divorced, suffering from adversity, taking early or later retirement, or advancing toward your earthly sunset—place your future with him and follow the rainbow of his promises.